THE NATIONAL ASSOCIATION OF
FLOWER ARRANGEMENT SOCIETIES

BOOK OF FLOWER ARRANGING

A STEP-BY-STEP GUIDE TO DECORATING YOUR HOME WITH FLOWERS

An arrangement of Staffordshire dogs posing beside an arrangement of *Gypsophilia paniculata* (baby's breath, chalk plant) and 'Bonny Jean' chrysanthemums (Arranger: Peggy Crooks).

THE NATIONAL ASSOCIATION OF
FLOWER ARRANGEMENT SOCIETIES

BOOK OF FLOWER ARRANGING

A STEP-BY-STEP GUIDE TO DECORATING YOUR HOME WITH FLOWERS

Compiled by Mary Newnes

EBURY PRESS
LONDON

ACKNOWLEDGEMENTS

Without the willing help of many people this book could not have been produced and on my own behalf, as well as for the National Association of Flower Arrangement Societies, I especially wish to thank the patient and hospitable owners of the homes where the flower arrangements were photographed: Mr and Mrs Buckingham, Mr and Mrs Peter Crooks, Lady Harriman and Mr and Mrs Arthur Watson. I also thank the owners of two houses which are open for the public to visit but which were made available outside these opening hours, Mr and Mrs John Warde of Squerryes Court in Kent and The National Trust for allowing us to use Wimpole Hall in Cambridgeshire. Sincere thanks are due also to Revd Canon N. J. Mantle MA for allowing flowers to be arranged and photographed in St John's Church, Rusthall, Kent.

To the willing and enthusiastic flower arrangers, just twenty from a membership of more than 100,000 gratitude is due for their willingness to share their skill and knowledge and their love of flowers. Their names appear alongside their arrangements. They would, in their turn, wish to thank all their good friends who cut flowers and foliage from their gardens or who lent special treasures. My additional thanks go to those who did so much preparatory work before the photography sessions, Peggy Crooks, Pearl Frost, Evelyn Mercer, Mary Watson and Mary Vander.

I do thank my husband for his encouragement and tolerance, and the officers of NAFAS for inviting me to compile this book on behalf of the Association.

Mary Newnes.

The publishers would like to thank Osborne and Little for the use of their fabrics for photography.

Editor: Suzanne Webber

Illustrators: Haywood & Martin

Photographer: Di Lewis

Published by Ebury Press, Division of The National Magazine Company Ltd, Colquhoun House 27–37 Broadwick Street, London WIV IFR

First Impression 1986
Second Impression 1986
Third Impression 1987
Fourth Impression 1988
Paperback edition 1988

ISBN 0 85223 431 7 (hardback)
     0 85223 721 9 (paperback)

Filmset by Advanced Filmsetters (Glasgow) Ltd
Printed and bound in Italy by New Interlitho, S.p.a., Milan

CONTENTS

INTRODUCTION

All the designs in this book are the work of well known flower arrangers. They may be consistent prize winners at shows, busy demonstrators, judges, teachers at further education classes, exhibitors at flower festivals, or committee members and administrators. Often they are involved in more than one of these activities but, whatever their interests within the organization of The National Association of Flower Arrangement Societies, they are agreed that one of their greatest pleasures is arranging flowers at home. From this starting point came the inspiration for this *Book of Flower Arranging*.

Their styles and ideas are as varied as the homes they live in and, although most of the arrangements are not shown in their own homes, in every case the setting inspired the design, the colours used and the scale and type of the plant material chosen by the arranger.

The arrangements were photographed through the year and reflect the wealth of material available in the summer, the richness of autumn, the party spirit of the winter months and the re-awakening growth of the spring.

Some of the designs draw attention to a favourite accessory or a group of treasures, not as these would be used in exhibits for competitive flower arranging but as they might be grouped at home. There are ideas, too, for flowers when entertaining, including wedding designs, both in church and at the reception.

Details, in a step-by-step form, of each arrangement have been included alongside the photographs. The containers, the accessories and the equipment needed are explained. In each case there is a brief description of the setting and the thoughts which led to the choice of the flowers and the way they were used and measurements are given so that it is possible to visualize the scale of each finished arrangement within its surroundings.

The plant material is named. Shown first is the name by which it will be found in most horticultural reference books and nurserymen's lists.

If there is a second name by which it is known this follows. The common names are given last. With these details it should be easy to find the same or similar plant material. Throughout the text the name which is most likely to be familiar has been used, for instance, hosta rather than plantain lily, alstromeria and not Peruvian lily; however, Solomon's Seal has been used and not polygonatum and forget-me-not appears rather than myosotis. Consistency in the use of either botanical or common names may appear to be desirable but in practice neither is entirely satisfactory.

No two arrangements can or should be identical. Meticulous copying is not the aim of this book and the line drawings and captions are intended for guidance and to answer some of the questions the less experienced arranger may wish to ask.

Inspiration comes from many sources and so, although it could appear helpful to include suggestions for similar containers, flowers, foliage, seedheads and so on, in place of those which have been chosen by the arrangers, it would not be a really useful addition. There are many subtle ways in which flowers hold their heads and leaves are joined to their stems and of surface texture and petal shape. Each arranger will find that a stem held in the hand will suggest shape and even movement and so a design will evolve. Without this inspiration from the flowers themselves arranging would soon lose its interest.

The ideas are here, they are a starting point for the reader's own pleasure in arranging flowers for the home.

I send my best wishes for the success of this delightful book, and my congratulations to the gifted arrangers, friends of many years. Their work is so beautifully illustrated that I am sure it will inspire many readers to practise this art and find it both rewarding and enjoyable.

Mary Tope. OBE, VMH,
FOUNDER PRESIDENT
OF NAFAS

FOR THE GUEST ROOM

IN THIS tiny arrangement there are some special plants picked from the garden for the enjoyment of a garden-loving visitor. It is designed for a bedroom window alcove. Everything is in scale, from the little figures to the tiny rosettes of sempervivum.

SIZE
20 cm × 15 cm (8 in × 6 in).

CONTAINER
A round, shallow tin, 6½ cm (2½ in) in diameter.

EQUIPMENT
A square of foam cut to fit across the tin firmly but also anchored with a plastic foam holder which is glued in the tin.

FOLIAGE
Viburnum farreri 'Nanum' ('Compactum').
Leptospermum cunninghamii (tea tree), leaves just breaking.
Lonicera nitida 'Baggesen's Gold' (box honeysuckle).
Tellima grandiflora (fringecup).
Conifer.
Pieris japonica (Andromeda japonica) 'Variegata'.
Sempervivum tectorum (houseleek).
Hedera helix (ivy).
Sedum spathifolium 'Purpureum'.

FLOWERS
Erica carnea (winter heather).
Galanthus elwesii (giant snowdrop).
G. viridapicis.
Skimmia 'Rubella'.
Gold-laced polyanthus.
Eranthis hyemalis (winter aconite).
Cornus mas (Cornelian cherry).
Berberis julianae (barberry).

ACCESSORIES
A pair of tiny cherub figures in a lead-coloured finish, mounted on strong wires. An oval piece of thin board, painted a dull green, 15 cm (6 in) long.

ARRANGER
Betty Treweeke

1 Place the tin to the left of the base and then add the figures, one on a longer wire in the centre, the other low down at the outer edge of the tin. Both should be facing towards the right. Take a curving stem of the viburnum and place it with its tip finishing just about 5 cm (2 in) above the head of the top figure. Put three graduated stems of leptospermum on the left, with a spray of heather below and more round the cherub on the right. Tuck a little lonicera in low on left and right. To give depth of colour and a background in the centre use two small tellima leaves. On the right, add sprays of the conifer where these, too, will provide a background for the flowers but take care to keep the daintiness of the outline.

2 Add the spray of variegated pieris leaves with its tiny buds in the centre, just covering the tin, and the bright yellow aconite flowers on either side. The tallest snowdrop should nod over the head of the top cherub, then thread the others through the centre of the arrangement. Add the rich red skimmia buds on the right, above the aconite and with three stems of *Cornus mas*, add more yellow out towards the left. Give the gold-laced polyanthus pride of place with two ivy leaves below.

3 Place a sprig of berberis buds behind the left-hand aconite. Finally, tuck small pieces of slate against the tin to hide it and take a few more along the line of the base board. Add the tiny houseleek rosettes so that they continue the line suggested by the figures.

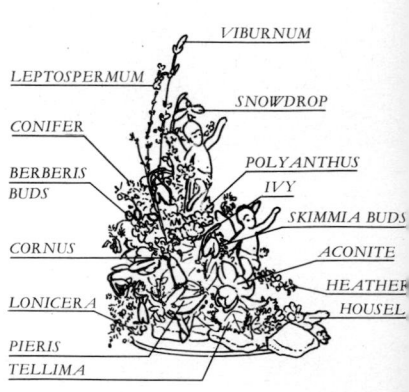

A Cottage Porch

THE WHITE walls and quarry tiles in the porch provide a simple setting for a few pot plants arranged in an interesting basket, its strong lines giving contrast to the design. The arrangement is a cheering welcome to visitors to the cottage.

SIZE
41 cm × 47 cm (16 in × 18½ in), including the handles.

CONTAINER
A split-cane, hinged basket used with a kitchen foil dish as a lining, 2 cm (¾ in) deep with sloping sides.

EQUIPMENT
A stone to weight the basket and to mask the dish.

PLANTS
FOLIAGE
Hedera helix 'Glacier' (ivy).
Peperomia magnoliaefolia (desert privet).
Nephrolepis exaltata (sword fern).

FLOWERS
Five pots of florists' polyanthus, two red, one pink and two yellow but all slightly different.

ARRANGER
Betty Treweeke

1 First give the plants a good watering before they are used. Place the basket in the corner of the window, put in the liner and then arrange a stone to hold it in position.

2 Put in the three foliage plants first, still in their pots, all lying on their sides against the edge of the dish. A more upright edge to a container would make them difficult to place at this angle. The ivy, with its more flowing lines when released from its supporting cane, is used at the front and the peperomia on the left, the fern on the right. If the pots tend to roll around, pebbles will make good chocks.

3 Take the polyanthus out of their pots and put them in polythene bags; they can be handled more easily this way and will fit between the foliage plants in their pots quite happily. Group the red and pink plants through the middle and use a yellow one on either side, the darker of the two yellow plants above the peperomia and the paler one in front of the fern and with a stem of the ivy drawn back between this plant and the red ones. All the pots and polythene bags should, by now, be invisible. If they still need camouflaging, a little moss can be added.

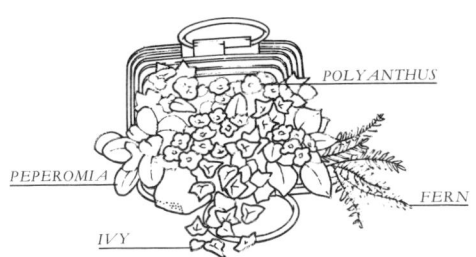

THE WHATNOT

A MIXTURE of fresh and preserved plant material is arranged on a 19th century whatnot, echoing the winter browns and greens of the garden seen through the open doorway. The delicate flowers on the branches of the witch hazel and the sunshine promise a change of season, from winter into spring.

SIZE
135 cm × 81 cm (178 cm from the floor) (53 in × 32 in).

CONTAINER
A round plastic dish 20 cm (8 in) in diameter.

EQUIPMENT
A block of wet foam attached to the bowl with tape.

FRESH MATERIAL
FOLIAGE
Rosmarinus officinalis (rosemary).
Camellia.
Euonymus japonicus medio-pictus.

FLOWERS
Branches of *Hamamelis × intermedia* 'Jelena' (witch hazel).
Garrya elliptica branches, with catkins.

DRIED MATERIAL
FOLIAGE
Eucalyptus gunnii (gum tree).
Mahonia japonica (leatherleaf).
Magnolia leaf.
Fagus sylvatica (common beech).

FLOWERS
Stems of the bracts of *Moluccella laevis* (bells of Ireland).
Made-up 'flowers' of wood shavings.
Protea cynaroides.

All the foliage and the moluccella are preserved with glycerine; the protea flower head is air dried.

ARRANGER
Kevin Gunnell

1 The outline is established by using the witch hazel first, an interesting twisting piece for the height and shorter pieces low down on either side to form a narrow triangular shape. Add a stem of eucalyptus on the right to emphasize the left-to-right flow of the design and a dark, shiny mahonia leaf to mark the centre of the arrangement and another to the left of it.

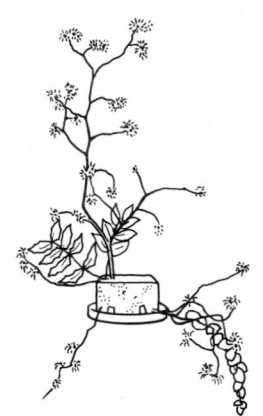

2 The pale cream moluccella stems are used next, strengthening the line of the witch hazel, both in the centre and, with two shorter pieces, on the left. Add the grey-green rosemary to curve up in the centre, just to the left of the moluccella, and then a spray of the garrya catkins on the left hand side. A second stem of the eucalyptus, shorter and placed a little higher and behind the first, will add depth. Reverse the one magnolia leaf to show its interesting colour and texture and place it to

come over the edge of the whatnot, to the left, at the front.

3 Next add the fresh camellia foliage in the centre, where its glossiness will contrast with the duller textures and paler colours all round it. Place more stems of the garrya to take its softer green up amongst the moluccella and out to the right. Add a richer colour with a few stems of the beech leaves at the front and on the left. A complete contrast of shape comes when the five wood shavings 'roses' are added to the design. Use the tallest quite high up in the arrangement and the lowest out to the right; this repeats the asymmetrical line once more. Just in front of the 'rose' in the centre front add a bright spray of euonymus for a highlight.

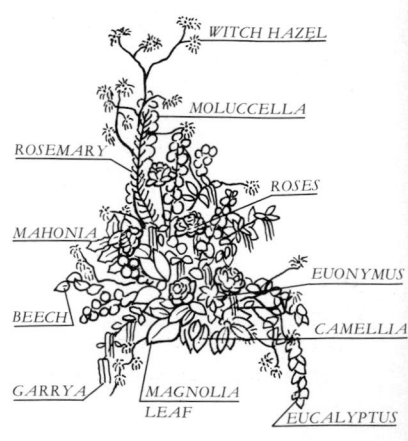

4 The finishing touch,
which seems
appropriate for a whatnot,
is to place the dried protea
flower head on the middle
shelf.

A PAPIER-MÂCHÉ chair, inlaid with mother-of-pearl, and a little table covered with a lace cloth, both of the nineteenth century, inspired an unusual arrangement.

The imaginative design suggests a fountain with the doves drinking there.

SIZE
122 cm × 74 cm (48 in × 29 in).

CONTAINER
A raised alabaster bowl complete with two doves, 23 cm high by 30½ cm in diameter (9 in × 12 in).

EQUIPMENT
Three small, round metal dishes, 3 cm (1 in) deep and 10 cm, 7½ cm and 6 cm in diameter (4 in, 3 in and 2⅓ in), are joined together by metal rods welded to their centres. (A DIY enthusiast could do this for you.) This 'stem' of containers is placed inside the bowl but raised up on a firmly anchored dry foam block so that the lowest of the three dishes is just below the rim of the bowl. Each dish has a square of well-soaked foam cut to fit and standing up above the rims by about 3 cm (1 in). Tape is taken across each dish once and, at the bottom, the whole structure is fixed to the bowl with another piece of tape going from side to side just in front of the rod.

FOLIAGE
Tsuga canadensis (Canadian hemlock).
Bergenia purpurascens (Megasea).
Hedera canariensis and *H.c.* 'Gloire de Marengo' (Canary Island ivy, green and variegated).
Helleborus foetidus (stinking hellebore).
Elaeagnus pungens 'Maculata'.
Mahonia japonica.
Ilex aquifolium 'Madame Briot' (holly).
Ligustrum ovalifolium 'Aureum' (privet).
Euonymus fortunei radicans (E. radicans) 'Emerald 'n Gold' (spindle family).

FLOWERS
Salix caprea (pussy willow).
Helleborus foetidus (stinking hellebore).
Helleborus orientalis (Lenten rose).
Hamamelis mollis (Chinese witch hazel).
Narcissus 'Paper White'.

ACCESSORIES
A stoneware yellow wagtail. A small silver box.

ARRANGER
Maureen Harrison

VICTORIANA

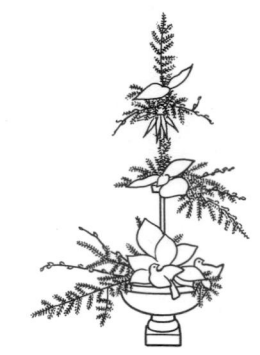

1 Working from the top, use the plant material so that it flows in alternate directions, first to the left, then right and then to the left again, getting wider sweeps as it is brought lower. The hemlock is the most important outline material so use this first. Take a slender spray to establish the height from the top dish and use similar pieces to mask the metal rods slightly, but keep the design light and with space between the three sections. Longer, curving sprays on one side are balanced by shorter and more bushy sprays on the other in each dish. Bergenia leaves come next. Two at the top, higher on the right than the left, three in the middle, all on the right hand side, and four in the lowest dish, to form a background for the dove in the front of the arrangement. One ivy leaf, showing its green veining against a purplish-brown which is similar to the colour of the bergenia leaves, will add unfussy interest here too. To complete the outline add curving pieces of pussy willow buds, to the left, the right and, again, the left, from the top downwards. Then add short stems of witch hazel, on the right at the top and the left at the bottom. One hellebore leaf added at the front of the top section will mask the rod without looking heavy.

2 Start adding more strength and colour to the design with three more ivy leaves, a greenish-brown one and a variegated one at the top and another variegated one in the middle, both coming down over the edges of the containers. The ivy leaves will be in a perpendicular line but this will be interesting and rather restful amongst the many different kinds and shapes of plant material. Put the little wagtail to the right of the arrangement and, to balance the suggestion of yellow feathers, add some stems of elaeagnus on the left. Carry this colour up to the middle but, this time, put a stem of elaeagnus towards the back on the right. Just below this last stem add a mahonia leaf, tucking it in under the front and lowest of the three bergenia leaves, following the downward line of the hemlock. On the left, follow this diagonal line with a short, bright piece of golden privet and, in the middle of the top section, a few clear yellow holly leaves. These will stand

out against the dark
roundness of the
bergenias.

3 Two sprays of the
green-flowered
hellebore and two stems of
the Lenten rose should be
added next, the pinkish
flowers in the top section,
one just on the left of the
tallest piece of hemlock
and the other on the right,
just under the topmost
bergenia leaf. The pale
green clusters of flowers
go into the middle and
lowest sections, one
slightly on the left in the
centre section and the
other, to the right, just
above the dove. Brightly
variegated euonymus is the
last kind of plant material
to be added to the three
parts of this arrangement.
It goes on the right at the
bottom, just under the
hellebore flowers in the
middle and there is a final,
tiny piece behind the holly
at the top.

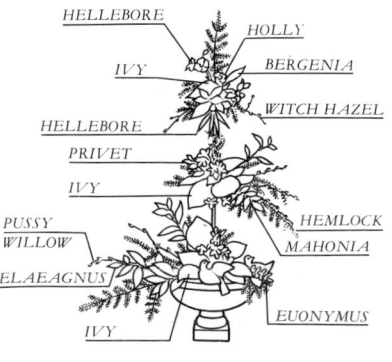

4 To complete the pic-
ture, open the little box
and put a few short stems
of the sweetly scented
'Paper White' narcissus,
held together loosely with
an elastic band, inside.
Their creamy colour will
suggest a link between the
whiteness of the doves and
the bright yellow of some
of the foliage.

SERENITY

THE CHINESE red of the background makes a delightful setting for this simple arrangement standing behind but incorporating the figure of an oriental lady. The slightly wind-swept movement of her dress has the same curving form as the opening spathes of the lilies and the pattern on the china repeats the warm red of the wall and the gold frame of the mirror.

SIZE
56 cm × 40 cm (22 in × 15¾ in).

CONTAINER
A small black bowl, 12 cm (4¾ in) in diameter. This stands on an oblong, carved, wooden stand, 20 cm long × 14 cm wide × 4 cm high (8 in × 5½ in × 1½ in).

EQUIPMENT
A pinholder anchored in the bowl with plasticine.

FOLIAGE
Aesculus hippocastanum (horse chestnut, buckeye), the unfurling leaves and buds.
Arum italicum 'Pictum'.

FLOWERS
Zantedeschia aethiopica (arum or calla lily).

ACCESSORY
White porcelain figure, 29 cm (11½ in) high.

ARRANGER
Peggy Crooks

1 The stand, with the bowl in its centre, is placed in a line parallel with the front of the chest, alongside but just in front of the group of china on the left.

Take two stems of horse chestnut to form the outline; the taller should curve very slightly to the left. Bring its top cluster of leaves directly over the bowl. Add the second and more curving short piece on the left, the tip curling round to the centre again and its leaves and buds suggesting a diagonal line towards the china.

2 Place the figure in front of the stand, centrally. Use the three lilies next. Their stems can be given graceful lines by holding them between the first fingers and thumbs of both hands and gently smoothing them into slight curves. Bring the first lily from behind the figure, up on the left, curving it very slightly in the opposite direction from the

chestnut, leaving the bloom in profile above the head of the figure. Curve the second one down to the right, slightly forward over the corner of the stand. The stem of the third lily should be a little shorter than the other two. Bring it out slightly to the left, just above the curving short piece of chestnut. Both the second and third lily should be turned a little more fully to the front than the first one.

3 Three *Arum italicum* leaves complete the picture. The first should be placed behind the lily on the left, framing it with dark green. Use the second, fractionally lower, on the right and the third to show off its marbled pattern as it comes forward on the right of the figure.

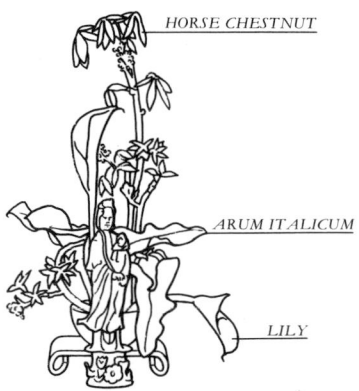

HORSE CHESTNUT

ARUM ITALICUM

LILY

COUNTRY KITCHEN

PINE FURNITURE, white walls and a collection of baskets, from which just two were chosen, suggested the style and content for this group of flowers, foliage, fruit and vegetables, assembled in the corner of the kitchen ready for informal entertaining.

SIZE
120 cm × 107 cm (47¼ in × 42 in).

CONTAINERS
A stoneware jug, 25 cm (10 in) tall and a stoneware casserole, 15 cm (6 in) across the opening. A small plastic dish, 9 cm (3 in) in diameter, inside a round basket, 18 cm (7 in) in diameter.

EQUIPMENT
Blocks of well-soaked foam, a tall piece wedged inside the jug, standing 5 cm (2 in) above the rim. The jug is first weighted with sand to the depth of about 8 cm (3 in). The casserole has a block of foam anchored on a pinholder and the dish inside the basket has foam fixed to a foam holder.

FOLIAGE
Sambucus racemosa 'Plumosa Aurea' (golden cut-leaved elder).
Rheum palmatum 'Atrosanguineum' (*R.p.* 'Rubrum') (ornamental rhubarb).

FLOWERS
Euphorbia robbiae (spurge—Miss Robb's bonnet).
Euphorbia myrsinites (spurge).
Helleborus orientalis hybrid (Lenten rose).
Yellow tulips, early single.

OTHER PLANT MATERIAL
Two grapefruit, three fresh artichoke heads, three bulbs of pinkish coloured garlic.

ACCESSORIES
Two baskets: a Sussex garden trug and a French market basket.

ARRANGER
Jean Deas

1 Group the jug, casserole and basket together in the angle of the pine washstand, the jug at the back, the casserole angled towards the left and lying on its side, the basket resting against the other two and facing to the right. Wedge the casserole and basket in place or use a putty substance to stop them rolling around. Weight the basket in position with a grapefruit placed in front of the foam. When using fruit it can be anchored in place with wooden cocktail sticks or wooden skewers. One cocktail stick will hold light-weight fruit in place; heavy fruit, like a pineapple, may need three or four sticks to hold it in the foam. Hang the baskets on the wall to the right of the pots, the round basket higher than the darker trug.

2 Work, first, with the elder. Take a tall, curved piece up from the jug to finish level with the rim of the top basket. Add another, shorter piece, to its right and another just below this. Take two longer stems and put these (still in the jug) below the trug and above the chair. The secondary stem of this last piece comes forward nearer to the centre of the arrangement. On the left use three more stems of elder, one towards the top, the next just below, almost on a line with the stem under the trug, and the third over the corner of the washstand. This last piece of elder comes out from the casserole, as does the next which comes forward over the edge of the stand, about halfway between the corner and the centre and then add the last piece, this time shorter, out from the jug, forward over the top of the casserole. Arrange two rheum leaves in the jug, the first up towards the right and the second down and also towards the right. Add two more rheum leaves, one hiding the stems of elder in the casserole and the other towards the back of the basket (this makes a background for a second grapefruit). To the right of the two grapefruit, place an artichoke, side view to the front. Add another artichoke between the basket and the casserole and a further one in the mouth of the casserole. Below the rheum leaf, on the left, group a few garlic bulbs.

3 Follow with stems of euphorbia, the bolder *E. robbiae* first. Use these round the arrangement, the stems shorter than the outlining elder, two on the left, one high and one low and two on the right, both towards the top and behind the elder. Nearer to the centre and running in a line from the left to low down on the right, place three stems of *Euphorbia myrsinites*. Use these three stems so that they will be recessed a little when the other flowers are added. (Singe the ends of the euphorbias before using them). Add next, to this inner part of the design, the hellebore flowers; their green and brownish-pink shades will pick up the colours of the rheum and the buds and stems of the elder. Tuck a hellebore in at the left-hand side of the grapefruit and another by the artichoke on the left.

4 The yellow tulips will pick up the colour of the grapefruit and, as they open with the warmth, they will add a completely different shape and petal texture to the arrangement. Use them to follow and highlight the inner placements of hellebores and euphorbias, towards the back on the left and right and then through the middle, down towards the grapefruit at the front.

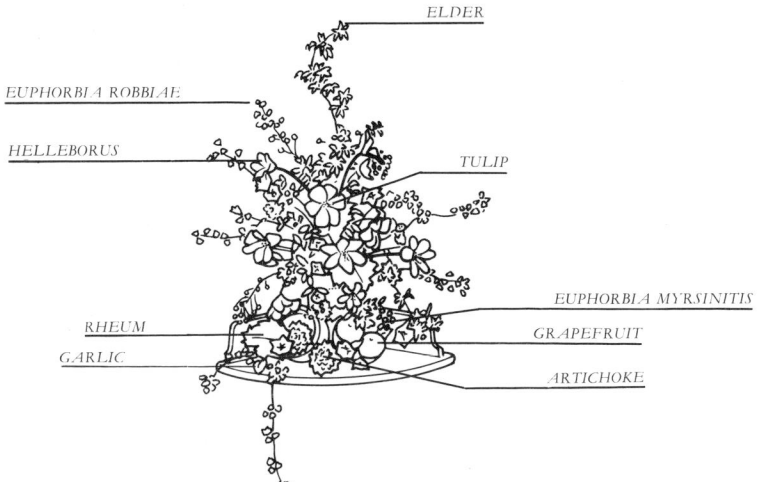

ELDER

EUPHORBIA ROBBIAE

HELLEBORUS

TULIP

EUPHORBIA MYRSINITIS

RHEUM

GARLIC

GRAPEFRUIT

ARTICHOKE

LILIES

AN INTEREST in the flower paintings of the French Impressionists inspired this arrangement of lilies. Their pure white, elegant, trumpet-shaped flowers, light green stems and slender leaves did not need any additional plant material and the glass goblet seemed the right container for the setting and the flowers.

SIZE
91 cm × 78 cm (36 in × 30¾ in).

CONTAINER
A modern Spanish glass goblet, 31 cm × 16 cm across the rim (12¼ in × 6½ in).

EQUIPMENT
A small piece of wire netting, 2½ cm (1 in) mesh, fitted across the back of the goblet.

FLOWERS
Six stems of *Lilium longiflorum* (Easter lily, white trumpet lily).

ACCESSORIES
Two Victorian Staffordshire jugs.

ARRANGER
Peggy Crooks

1 Fix a small piece of wire netting very securely to the back half of the goblet. Do this by taking the cut ends of the wire and hooking them over the rim.

Slight variations in stem lengths are necessary but do not cut any too short or their elegance will be lost. The shape and colour of the leaves is important so let as many as possible remain on the stems. They will help to mask the wire and the finished arrangement will appear to have been created without any equipment.

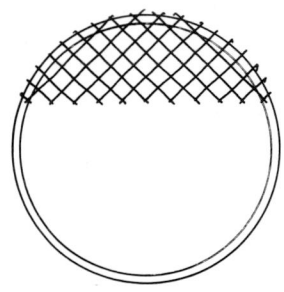

2 With the two tallest stems, establish the height at the back of the arrangement, one stem just a little higher than the other. Support them in the wire. Take the third stem to the left, again putting it through the wire but angled so that it rests against the rim of the goblet. The fourth stem balances its weight by being used just below the second, on the right, and turned a little to lean towards the back. This also means the reverse of

the flowers can be seen and enjoyed. On the right, place a stem to come quite low down and then a shorter one, which is not put through the wire, to come forward in the middle of the design. Rest the stem on the right against the rim of the goblet but keep the central one just above it and make sure that when this last stem is put in position it does not disturb the other five.

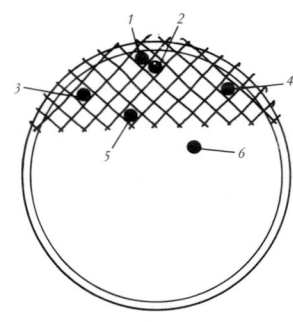

3 Add the jugs. There are interesting colour links between the jugs, the setting and the flowers. The outer matt finish blends with the furnishings and the inner, glazed, finish repeats the whiteness of the flowers.

ORIENTAL BLOSSOM

THE PAINTINGS, the vase, the carved wooden stand and the cane-handled teapot are grouped together with a charming simplicity which makes good use of space and the clarity of line so often shown in oriental designs. The pictures of blossom inspired the arrangement and the sweeping diagonal line follows their position on the wall, leading on to the teapot standing to the right on the table.

SIZE
103 cm × 78 cm (41 in × 30¾ in).

CONTAINER
Chinese vase, 25 cm × 14 cm (10 in × 5½ in). Carved stand, 7 cm high (2¾ in).

EQUIPMENT
A little wire-netting, crumpled and wedged with care in the neck of the vase.

FOLIAGE
Only that on the flower stems.

FLOWERS
Prunus × hillieri 'Spire' (ornamental cherry).
Camellia japonica, rose-formed (large formal double), in pale pink and deep pink.

ACCESSORY
Chinese teapot.

ARRANGER
Jean Deas

1 Use the cherry blossom first. Bring a tall, branching piece out from the left of the vase and curve the tip in towards the top of the higher picture. Take a shorter piece out to the right, almost horizontally, over the rim of the vase, its secondary shoot leading backwards a little towards the wall and a spray of its blossom falling forward over the front edge. With a shorter, third stem complete the outline. Put this at the back and angle it towards the wall from left to right.

2 Take the camellias and use them in a curve from left to right, following the lower lines of the blossom stems. The glossy dark green leaves make an important background for the flowers against the pale wall. Place one deep pink camellia below the cherry on the left and one just above the lowest stem on the right, both facing outwards. Next take two, fully open,

pale pink flowers and use the larger, facing forward, in front of the cherry and the dark bloom on the right. Place the other on the left and a little nearer the centre of the arrangement, also facing forward.

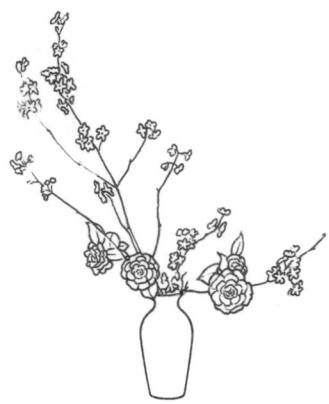

3 With one more, fully open camellia, this time a dark one, follow the line of the right-hand stem of cherry which leads towards the wall. This flower should look upwards between the pictures. Take two pale pink buds and place one just above the spray of cherry blossom in the centre of the arrangement and the other facing upwards at the back of the arrangement on the left. The teapot continues the diagonal line formed, in the first place, by the pictures.

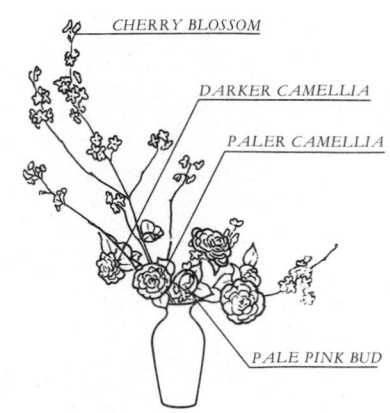

CHERRY BLOSSOM

DARKER CAMELLIA

PALER CAMELLIA

PALE PINK BUD

AN UNUSUAL arrangement which uses colour with particularly successful results. The pale cream lilies are only fractionally darker than the background but including their own, dark green, slender leaves has given these flowers definition without adding any heaviness to the design. The copper colour of the stamens is repeated in the markings on the petals of the alstroemerias and, again, in some of the foliage. The lily-buds add a lively touch of lime green, picked up by the foliage in the little arrangement and the bronze figures continue the colour theme of cream to rich brown.

SIZE
94 cm × 58½ cm (37 in × 23 in).
19 cm × 8 cm (8 in × 3 in) for the small arrangement.

CONTAINERS
An early 19th century Limoges candelabra, 35½ cm × 28 cm (14 in × 11 in), placed on a wooden base, 4 cm (1½ in) high.
A small tin, 9 cm (3½ in) diameter.

EQUIPMENT
Two candle-cup holders, covered in cream ribbon, and blocks of well-soaked foam, cut to fit and taped in position, standing 4 cm (1½ in) above the rim of the holders.
A block of wet foam in the tin, standing 2½ cm (1 in) above the rim.

FOLIAGE
Spiraea japonica 'Goldflame'.
Nandina domestica (heavenly bamboo).
Lily stems.
Hosta fortunei 'Aureomarginata' (plantain lily).
Tellima grandiflora (T. odorata) (fringecup).

FLOWERS
Lilium 'Sterling Silver' (lily).
Alstroemeria 'Ligtu Hybrids' (Peruvian lily).

ACCESSORIES
A pair of bronze figures, on wooden bases which are 4 cm (1½ in) high, one figure placed a little behind the other and to the right.

ARRANGER
Sylvia Lewis

FOR AN ALCOVE

1 Stand the candelabra centrally in the alcove with the bronzes on its left. Form the outline with two slender stems of spiraea foliage, evenly matched and placed in the centre of each candle-cup holder. Place short, graceful stems of nandina leaves to come out and down a little on both sides.

2 Add shorter pieces of spiraea in the middle of both parts of the design and then nandina below the first pieces and out towards the front, just linking the two halves of the arrangement together above the candelabra figure. Place tall stems of lilies with very tight buds at the top of both (by the first stems of spiraea) and then add more lily-buds on either side of the arrangement, about halfway down. With alstroemerias follow the lines of the nandina, also taking some across the middle above the figure. Take four dark-leaved lily stems and, with two, follow the upright lines of the first spiraea

stems, finishing about 15 cm (6 in) lower. Add two slightly shorter stems towards the outside.

3 Towards the back and just coming down over the candle-cups, place two hosta leaves; these should not be seen from the front but will mask the foam and holders from the side views. Add the lilies, bringing them from the outside towards the centre on both sides of the arrangement, just opening flowers at the top and fully open in the centre. Towards the outside, on both right and left, add a few more stems of half-open lilies and their buds.

4 For the small arrangement, form a setting
for a few short stems of
spiraea foliage and five
alstroemeria flower heads
with three small tellima
leaves. Group these in
rosette form in the middle
of the foam which stands
in the tin. Then place the
other plant material so that
it is highest at the back on

the left, forming a diagonal
line with the tallest point
coming between the
bronze figures and the
candelabra.

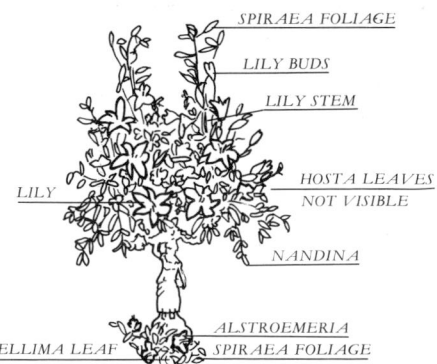

SPIRAEA FOLIAGE

LILY BUDS

LILY STEM

HOSTA LEAVES
NOT VISIBLE

LILY

NANDINA

ALSTROEMERIA
TELLIMA LEAF   SPIRAEA FOLIAGE

25

COLOUR HARMONY

THIS ARRANGEMENT stands on a small side table by an attractive 18th century corner cupboard. The position of the gilt-framed Victorian picture and the furniture suggested the design. The dusky pink colours in the furnishings and the gold of the picture frame suggested the colours for the arrangement. Pale green, orange-gold, yellow and darker green together provide a background for many shades of pink.

SIZE
71 cm × 101 cm wide (28 in × 40 in).

CONTAINER
*Round pewter bowl on small feet,
20 cm × 7½ cm deep (8 in × 3 in).*

EQUIPMENT
One block of foam, the greater part fitted across the middle of the bowl, the remainder cut to fit in front, both parts standing 7½ cm (3 in) above the rim and taped together across the bowl from front to back.

FOLIAGE
Jasminum officinale 'Affine' (jasmine, jessamine).
Stephanandra tanakae.
Cotoneaster conspicuus 'Decorus'.
Spiraea japonica 'Goldflame'.
Hosta fortunei 'Albopicta' ('Picta')
(plantain lily).

FLOWERS
Weigela florida 'Variegata' *(Diervilla florida).*
Antirrhinum majus (snapdragon).
Primula pulverulenta 'Bartley Strain'.
Endymion hispanicus (Scilla campanulata, S. hispanica) (Spanish bluebell).
Lilium 'Rosita'.
Alstroemeria 'Ligtu Hybrids' (Peruvian lily).
Ranunculus asiaticus (Persian buttercup, turban ranunculus).

ARRANGER
Edna Johnson

1 With the container placed two-thirds of the way back and to the left of the table, make the outline of the arrangement with the jasmine, stephanandra and cotoneaster. Use graceful stems of the jasmine to curve towards the picture, the tallest just to its left. Take three stems of cotoneaster and use this darker green material on the right, still at the back of the container, and then one more stem over on the left but low down in the arrangement. Take two sprays of the stephanandra and place one at either side, over the edge of the table towards the front on the left, towards the back on the right. Add a few stems of the richly coloured spiraea foliage, following the lines of the jasmine stems but not so tall.

2 Create more depth in the centre of the arrangement, first with the hosta leaves. Use two to the right of the centre and coming forward and down a little, three more, with longer stems, up towards the tallest piece of jasmine, then add more pieces of spiraea, bringing them forward and out a little to the right and the left. At both sides of this central group and towards the back of the arrangement add some stems of the variegated weigela with its pale pink flowers.

3 Strengthen the outline by adding pink antirrhinums, the tallest up near the tallest stem of jasmine, the shortest low down and coming forward over the table to the right of the centre, five more between them on the right and three, rather shorter stems, on the left. Add the primulas next, their stems slightly shorter than the antirrhinums, placing them from just to the left of the centre through to the right. Use the bluebells on the left, in and out among the foliage. Both the primulas and the bluebells are dainty in form but contribute important colour notes to the design.

4 The lilies are beautiful at every stage, from tight bud when they are pale green, to fully open when they become a peach-pink, so use them to show their changing shapes and colours. Place a half-open bud near the top of the arrangement and another at the centre front, some fully open blooms in the middle and graceful green buds following the lines of the design. To do this successfully keep the stems of lilies quite long and this will allow their graceful form to show against the background of the hosta leaves and spiraea stems, some of the spiraea will be in among the sprays of lilies now. Finally, place a few alstroemeria blooms in among the lilies and add a stronger pink with the papery-looking ranunculus. Apart from the change of colour, they are quite different in form with their many petals. Bring them through the middle and then add one out to the left, near the dark green of the stephanandra leaves, and another in profile, high up, to the right of the centre, where it contrasts with antirrhinum, lily, lily-bud and primula, completing the colourful and harmonious arrangement of rich pinks, golds and greens.

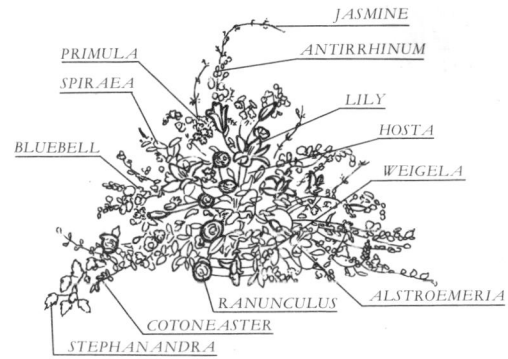

PRIMULA
JASMINE
ANTIRRHINUM
SPIRAEA
LILY
BLUEBELL
HOSTA
WEIGELA
RANUNCULUS
ALSTROEMERIA
COTONEASTER
STEPHANANDRA

THE RICH colours of the azaleas may seem a surprising choice for the arrangement in this bedroom with its very pale pink walls but here is an example of how colours can be blended together successfully. The skill is in using the correct quantities of each shade and knowing just where to place the strong colours in the arrangement. The azaleas, mixed with the soft peach-pink lilies, are kept towards the middle, while most of the very pale pink, cream and white flowers are used with the outline material.

The china basket chosen for this arrangement goes beautifully with the delicate, painted, cast-iron whatnot and the arrangement is, despite its size, delicate and charming.

SIZE
119 cm × 101½ cm (47 in × 40 in).

CONTAINER
China basket, 33½ cm × 23½ cm wide × 9 cm deep, excluding the handle (13¼ in × 9¼ in × 3½ in).
The whatnot stands 71 cm high × 40½ cm wide (28 in × 16 in).

EQUIPMENT
Block of foam, standing above the rim 5 cm (2 in) at the handle. This is taped across twice, once on either side of the handle.

FOLIAGE
Athyrium felix-femina (lady fern, glade fern).
Sorbus aria (whitebeam).
Helleborus orientalis (Lenten rose).

FLOWERS
Lonicera periclymenum 'Belgica' (early Dutch honeysuckle, woodbine).
Jasminum officinale (common jasmine, jessamine).
Deutzia pulchra.
Hydrangea petiolaris (climbing hydrangea).
Wisteria venusta.
Deciduous rhododendrons (azaleas).
Lilium 'Rosita' and Lilium 'Sentinel'.

ARRANGER
Edna Johnson

AZALEAS

1 All the outline material is very curving and pretty and this gives delicacy to the finished design. The arrangement is seen as you come into the room, to its left, as well as from the front. To establish the height, take a piece of honeysuckle up to the right, curving towards the centre, and then add another piece, shorter, below it on the right, Add more curving sprays, this time of jasmine, three sweeping down on the left and two, slightly shorter pieces, on the right. Among the jasmine, towards the back on the left and in front of it on the right, add stems of the deutzia and one piece just to the left of the taller stem of honeysuckle, curving over the line of the basket's handle.

towards the back of the arrangement. Next take three pieces of the grey-leafed whitebeam and place the tallest between the honeysuckle and the deutzia in the middle, still creating the outline and working from the back third of the block of foam. Just below it, add a second piece, curving to the left, and a third quite low down, its tip continuing the very gentle S-shaped outline formed from the top of the tallest stem of honeysuckle, through the tips of the three stems of whitebeam and finishing along the curve of the jasmine on the outside left. If this 'waisted' line is lost the arrangement will be too rounded and heavy-looking when it is complete.

2 Add two elegant ferns, low down on the right, another towards the front, the next out at the back on the right and the fifth going from just to the left of the handle out

3 Take five hellebore leaves and place these palmate, slightly shiny, dark green leaves in the middle of the design, two, overlapping a little, down towards the left, two more towards the right at the front and one in front of the tallest piece of white-beam. Next, add two of the white hydrangea heads against this green back-ground and two more to come forward over the edge of the whatnot. Add a fifth one, low in the arrangement and round towards the back on the right. With the addition of a few graceful heads of the white wisteria, also falling forward over the edge on the right-hand side, and another, higher, in front of the shorter stem of the honeysuckle, this stage of the arrangement is com-plete.

4 Add the colourful azaleas next, the paler nearer the outside. Choose a well shaped spray of flowers and place it well down, slightly towards the front on the left, then another longer stem to show through behind the honeysuckle. Add another towards the back on the right, half hidden from the front view, and a fourth, also half hidden, flowing out towards the wall at the back on the left. Place the brighter azaleas nearer the centre of the arrangement on both sides and then link

the two sides together with pink lilies threaded through the arrangement from the right down to the left. Accent the outline by adding some long, graceful stems of the pale lilies with their creamy-green buds and half open flowers.

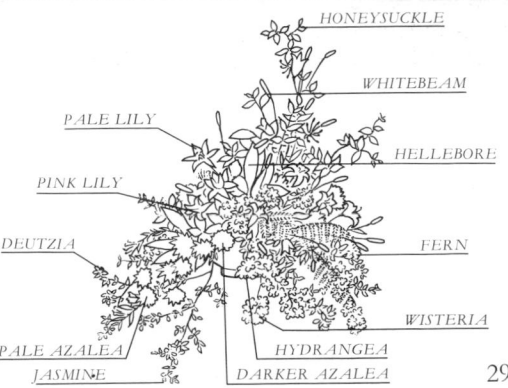

IDEAS SUGGESTED by the paintings of the Flemish School can be seen here in the way the mixed flowers, with their rich colours and varied forms, have been used, but this is very much a design of today and it would make an attractive decoration for a sherry party. It picks up the colours of sherry from pale and dry to dark, rich and sweet and the group of fruit and glass adds to the 'still life' theme.

SIZE
78¾ cm × 68½ cm (31 in × 27 in).

CONTAINER
An ornate silver-plated stand with a flat, circular top, 24 cm × 28 cm (9½ in × 11 in) in diameter at the top.

EQUIPMENT
A round pottery dish, 20 cm (8 in) in diameter, 5 cm (2 in) deep. Half a block of well-soaked foam held in place with two strong rubber bands over the foam and the dish.

FOLIAGE
Fagus sylvatica 'Roseomarginata' (a purple-leaved beech).
Grevillea robusta (silk oak).
Leucothoe fontanesiana (L. catesbaei, Andromeda catesbaei) (dog hobble, fetterbush).

FLOWERS
Freesia refracta 'Midas'.
Alstroemeria 'Ligtu Hybrids'.
Lilium szovitsianum, yellow and cream.
Rose 'Mercedes'.
Iris, Dutch hybrid.
Carnations, perpetual flowering florists' variety, lemon-yellow with orange tips. Pale pink spray carnations.
Allium rosenbachianum.

FRUIT
Grapes, orange and apple.

ACCESSORY
Silver coaster with fruit.

ARRANGER
Winifred Simpson

FINO

1 A triangular outline is formed with the beech, leucothoe and grevillea. Use the beech at both sides curving down towards the dresser and a third branching spray of leaves just to the left of an imaginary central line. Next use the leucothoe, three stems, one on the right in front of the beech and the other two on the left, also in front of the beech. Take two stems of grevillea and place these to curve towards the right at the top of the arrangement, one shorter and a little in front of the other but turning out towards the wall.

inner triangle, the two lowest stems by the leucothoe on either side, two more, higher and nearer the centre, another up on the left and then, at the top, a pink-splashed flower above the central freesia and in front of the top leaf of the beech. Above this last flower place two stems of the bright yellow lily and another out to its left.

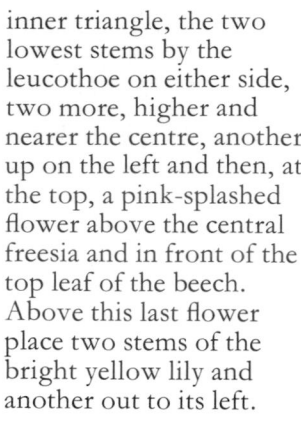

2 With the long-stemmed yellow freesias add to the outline material, in the middle, on the left, and low to the right. Place another freesia lower on the left and a final one coming forward slightly just above the foam in the middle of the arrangement. Add six stems of alstroemeria, suggesting an

3 Between the top lilies place a red rose, slightly to the right. On the left and a little higher place the one blue iris, turning the flower head in towards the lily to follow the line of the grevillea, avoiding the top of the arrangement becoming too broad. Add another rose to the right of the pink alstroemeria. On the left, between the two freesias, add the three orange-tipped yellow carnations with a spray of the pale pink carnations above the two lower blooms and another pink spray of carnations on the right between the two alstroemerias.

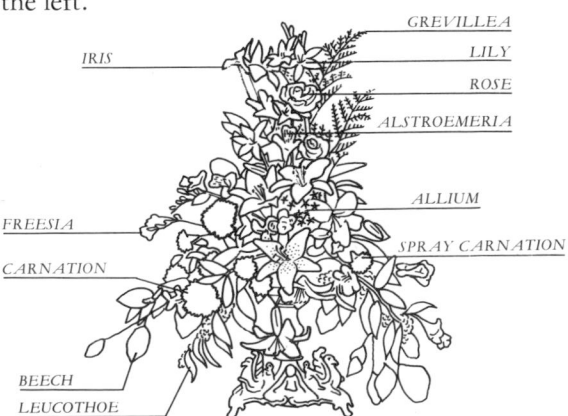

their buds, in a curve below the second red rose. Behind the middle of these lilies place the one allium head with its little purple star-like flowers contrasting with the smooth lily petals. Below, and in the centre of the arrangement, add the cream lily with a spray of pink carnations on its left. Behind this cream flower and facing down towards the dresser add two more yellow lilies.

hand side, the orange and apple in the front and the bunch of black grapes behind and coming out to the left.

4 Continue to add stems of lilies, more fully open flowers than those used before, three, with

5 Put the coaster in front of the arrangement, just to the right-

SUMMER BOUQUET

THE GRACEFUL asymmetrical curves of this beautiful summer bouquet contrast with the pattern formed by the leaded lights of the window, beyond are the colours and shapes of the garden. Delicate sprays of blossom have been skilfully used to give a sense of movement. Without them this centrally-placed arrangement would have been a pleasure to look at but rather conventional in its static triangular shape.

SIZE
104 cm × 76 cm wide (41 in × 30 in).

CONTAINER
A pink and white china compote, 24 cm × 18 cm high (9½ in × 7 in).

EQUIPMENT
A block of well-soaked foam, cut to fit across the dish and anchored on a foam holder fixed to the dish.

FOLIAGE
Hosta elata (plantain lily).
Hosta fortunei 'Albopicta' (*H.f.* 'Picta') (plantain lily).
Jasminum officinale 'Aureovariegata' (variegated jasmine, jessamine).

FLOWERS
Deutzia pulchra.
Deutzia × rosea.
Cherry blossom, late flowering.
Choisya ternata (Mexican orange blossom).
Syringa vulgaris (lilac).
Viburnum opulus (guelder rose, Whitsun bosses).
Antirrhinum majus (snapdragon).
Alstroemeria 'Ligtu Hybrids' (Peruvian lily).
Wisteria venusta.
Lilium 'Rosita' (lily).
Pink spray carnations—florists'.
Pink roses—florists'.

ARRANGER
Edna Johnson

1 Place the first stem of pink deutzia in the centre of the container, taking the curving tip over to the right. To give immediate visual balance, use heavily flowered pieces out to the right and the left—long and low. Add shorter curving, pieces above them. Complete the outline, keeping the slightly asymmetrical shape, with both pink and white deutzia and a few stems of the single cherry blossom, three on the right and one low on the left.

2 Form a rosette of foliage in the centre with the hosta leaves. Group the variegated ones towards the left and then use the two plain green leaves on the right, the first coming over the front of the dish and the second just above it but out and down more to the right. Behind these leaves add some choisya with its dark green foliage and sweetly scented white flowers. Then add the lilac. Place a stem low down on the left, finishing just above the sill. Put a second stem out to the right, almost forming a diagonal line with the first across the arrangement. Below this second stem add a spray of guelder rose bosses to come right forward over the edge of the sill and then add a few of the twisting, dainty stems of variegated jasmine on either side of the arrangement.

3 Still keeping the original outline, add stems of antirrhinums towards the outside and place some of the alstroemerias, a few single blooms, low down just to the right of the centre, a longer stem out to the right and another high up on the left. Below the lilac, on the left and halfway up on both sides, add racemes of the dainty wisteria.

4 Complete the arrange-
ment by filling in the
centre, but as you do this
make sure that some
flowers are recessed and
others brought forward a
little, keeping a light
effect, showing off each
flower against its neigh-
bours. Use alstroemerias,
lilies and spray carnations
blended together through
the middle with the
brighter pink roses added
last.

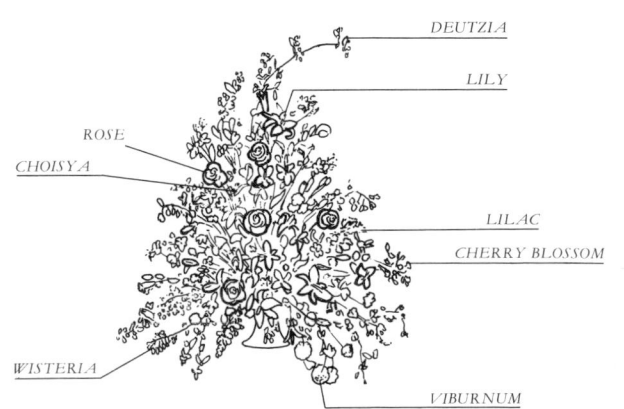

DEUTZIA

LILY

ROSE

CHOISYA

LILAC

CHERRY BLOSSOM

WISTERIA

VIBURNUM

ROSES AND A DRESDEN FIGURE

S TANDING ON a side table in an entrance hall, the Dresden candlestick, with its dainty figure and pink and green decoration, holds aloft an arrangement which picks up its colours. Light-textured flowers among the roses contrast with the hosta leaves and the arrangement is reflected attractively in the mirror.

SIZE
91½ cm from the table × 61 cm
(36 in × 24 in).

CONTAINER
A Dresden candlestick, 40½ cm × 20 cm
(16 in × 8 in).

EQUIPMENT
A candle-cup holder with a block of well-soaked foam cut to fit and standing 8 cm (3 in) above its rim, the foam taped to the candle-cup and then to the candlestick.

FOLIAGE
Hosta 'Thomas Hogg' (plantain lily).

FLOWERS
Tellima grandiflora (T. odorata)
(fringecup).
Rose 'Bridal Pink'.
Euphorbia cyparissias (spurge).

ARRANGER
Sylvia Lewis

1 Place the candlestick in front of the mirror, at a slight angle, the figure looking towards the door. Take a tall stem of tellima and place this three-quarters of the way back in the foam, curving its tip slightly to the left. Add a second stem just to its left. Make a clear outline with rose-buds from the top and down on both sides, finishing with a bud lower on the right than the left. Next, take three half-open roses and put them in the centre, one about half-way up the arrangement, one directly below it and out to the front, over the edge of the holder, the third between these two but on the right.

2 Working from this framework, place the hosta leaves in a group through the middle of the arrangement, starting with one near the highest of the last three roses, leading out to the left, the next under the rose and to its right,

the third, again towards the right, this time below the last rose to be placed. With two more hosta leaves frame the lowest of the three roses, one out

more short pieces of tellima tucked in towards the sides and the back.

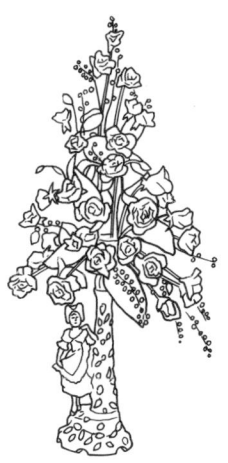

3 Add more roses, remembering to take some round to the side and the back where they will be seen when passing and also be reflected in the mirror. Complete the arrangement with stems of yellow-green euphorbia, mostly recessed a little beside the roses.

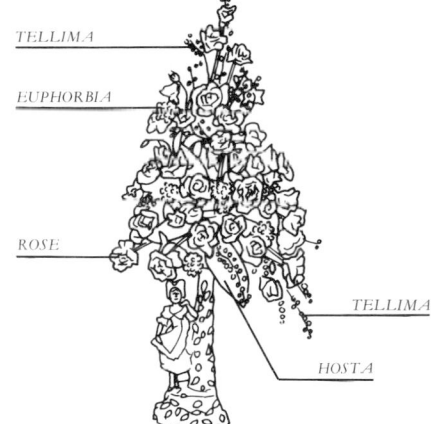

TELLIMA

EUPHORBIA

ROSE

TELLIMA

HOSTA

towards the left and the other from just below and to its right. At the back and side of the arrangement, use two or three small hosta leaves to mask the foam but do not let them show from the front. Add three stems of tellima behind the lowest rose-bud on the right to curve down towards the table. Use

LEAVES FROM A SUMMER GARDEN

A N ORIENTAL bronze urn, filled with richly-coloured foliage, stands on a 17th century Indo-Portuguese chest, with Spanish embroidered pictures on either side and 18th century panelling behind. The arrangement, with its contrast of finely cut and bold shining leaves and its touches of golden yellow and white, complements the setting and does not, in any way, compete with it.

SIZE
61 cm × 46 cm (24 in × 18 in).

CONTAINER
Bronze urn 40½ cm high (16 in), standing on a round dark wooden base 2 cm (¾ in) deep.

EQUIPMENT
Block of soaked foam, standing 7½ cm (3 in) above the rim, covered with 5 cm (2 in) mesh wire attached to the handles of the urn.

FOLIAGE
Berberis thunbergii 'Atropurpurea' (purple-leaved Japanese barberry) and *B.t.* 'Rose glow'.
Acer palmatum 'Atropurpureum' (purple-leafed Japanese maple).
Philadelphus coronarius 'Aureus' (golden-leafed mock orange blossom).
Pieris formosa forrestii 'Wakehurst' (*Andromeda formosa*).

FLOWERS
Gypsophila paniculata 'Bristol fairy' (baby's breath, chalk plant).

ARRANGER
Evelyn Mercer

1 Stand the urn on the base. This is chosen to be as unobtrusive as possible and is used to protect the chest. Form the outline of the arrangement with *Berberis thunbergii* 'Atropurpurea' at the top and graceful sprays of acer leaves, two on the left, one on the right and a shorter one towards the back just to the right of the berberis. Add the bright gold philadelphus between the two stems of acer and leading out towards the pictures on the left, and another on the right coming forward over the edge of the urn. These stems of philadelphus are used for the brilliant colour of their foliage but their less significant white flowers will link attractively with the gypsophila.

2 Add more berberis, shorter stems of both 'Atropurpurea' and 'Rose Glow', in the middle and to the right. Then, starting with a tall piece, place three pieris stems to come from just to the left of the tallest berberis through to the front of the arrangement. Add another stem of pieris high on the right.

3 Delicate sprays of gypsophila flowers complete the arrangement. Use them with discretion. Take stems, which are a little shorter than the outline berberis and acer, and add their contrast of form and scale outside the pieris, leaving the glowing colour and shining surfaces of these leaves to show clearly.

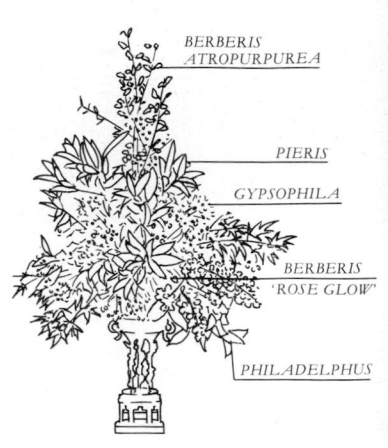

BERBERIS ATROPURPUREA

PIERIS

GYPSOPHILA

BERBERIS 'ROSE GLOW'

PHILADELPHUS

TRAVELLER'S JOY

ONE LOVELY clematis flower started the quest for the right container and complementary companions. This delightful arrangement for the guest room is the result.

SIZE
48½ cm × 48 cm (19½ in × 19 in).

CONTAINER
A china sugar-pot with cover
16½ cm × 23 cm (6½ in × 9 in) across the handles.

EQUIPMENT
A pinholder holding a block of soaked foam standing 6½ cm (2½ in) above the rim of the bowl.

FOLIAGE
Nephrolepsis exaltata 'Bostoniensis' (Boston fern).
Plectranthus (Swedish ivy).
Pittosporum tenuifolium 'Garnettii'.
Polygonatum × hybridum (P. multiflorum) (Solomon's seal).
Thalictrum minus (lesser meadow rue).
Rhododendron, a variegated-leaved form.
Cyrtomium falcatum (holly or fishtail fern).

FLOWERS
Tellima grandiflora (T. odorata) (fringecup).
Euphorbia polychroma (E. epithymoides) (spurge).
Alstroemeria 'Ligtu Hybrids' (Peruvian lily).
Spray carnations.
Allium rosenbachianum.
Clematis 'Nelly Moser'.

OTHER PLANT MATERIAL
Grasses, dried and fresh, wild.

ARRANGER
Winifred Simpson

1 With the sugar-pot in place, put the lid to rest against its foot on the left-hand side; here it will complete a line of colour running from right to left in the arrangement. Form the outline with three fronds of the Boston fern, one to each side and one in the middle, establishing the height. Use this last frond in profile so that the line is very slender. Low on the right use a spray of plectranthus foliage and, below this a short stem of the pink-edged pittosporum. Add grasses and stems of tellima on either side of the tallest fern and, on the right, a stem of Solomon's seal leaves. To the left, just over the rim of the pot, place a stem of thalictrum leaves almost touching the lid. Just above this stem add a rosette of leaves from the variegated rhododendron.

2 Take a second rosette of the rhododendron and put it in the foam to the left of the Solomon's seal; here it will form a good central background, stopping too much light coming through from the window but, because of its variegation, it will not look heavy. Take a second stem of pittosporum out to the back and, in the very front, place a small piece of the euphorbia to come over the rim of the pot. To its right, add another frond of the Boston fern with a slightly shorter and darker holly-fern stem in front. One more stem of the elegant grass towards the back on the right completes this stage.

3 Both shades of the alstroemeria are added now, the paler at the top on the left and also down to the far right. Two darker flowers follow; put one quite low in the arrangement on the right and the second just to the left of the euphorbia. Above and below the darker shaded alstroemeria on the right, place small, pale pink carnations and then add another on the left above the first piece of rhododendron. Complete the arrangement with one reddish-purple allium in front of the Solomon's seal leaf, the mauve and carmine-red clematis flower below it and looking just a little to the left.

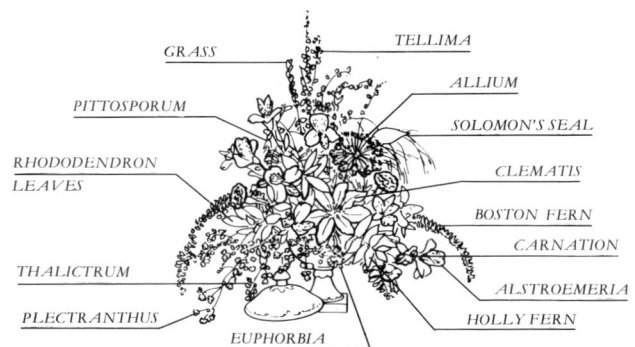

GRASS

TELLIMA

PITTOSPORUM

ALLIUM

SOLOMON'S SEAL

RHODODENDRON
LEAVES

CLEMATIS

BOSTON FERN

CARNATION

THALICTRUM

ALSTROEMERIA

PLECTRANTHUS

HOLLY FERN

EUPHORBIA

POT-POURRI

PLUMP LITTLE Victorian cherubs enjoy an elegant pot-pourri of flowers and foliage. The fresh green of the ferns and grasses picks up the green of the wall and the colours in the curtain are found again in the flowers.

SIZE
94 cm × 68½ cm (37 in × 27 in).

CONTAINER
A Victorian lamp base, 33 cm × 18 cm (13 in × 7 in).

EQUIPMENT
A block of soaked foam fitting across the bowl top, taped in place.

FOLIAGE
Fagus sylvatica 'Roseomarginata' (a purple-leaved beech).
Larix kaempferi (L. leptolepis) (Japanese larch).
Polystichum setiferum (P. angulare) (a soft shield fern or hedge fern).
Grevillea robusta (silk oak).

FLOWERS
Euphorbia cyparissias (spurge).
Spray carnations, florists' variety.
Carnations, perpetual flowering florists' variety.
Dicentra spectabilis (bleeding heart).
Alstroemeria 'Ligtu Hybrids' (Peruvian lily).
Allium karataviense.
Allium rosenbachianum.
Orchid, florists' variety.
Rose, florists' variety.

OTHER PLANT MATERIAL
Various wild grasses.

ACCESSORIES
Shells and pot-pourri.

ARRANGER
Winifred Simpson

1 Two stems of the pink-edged purple beech, one placed at either side of the cherubs, have deep colour and bold shapes which will unify the design as it stands between two very different backgrounds. Place a tall stem of grass just to the left of the curtain edge and establish the finished height with this stem. Above the beech, on the left, add three short, bright green stems of larch and above them two ferns, the lower one turned a little towards the back. On the right, above the beech, add another fern and then a fourth behind and to the right of the grass. In front of this last fern place a stem of grevillea, curving from the centre out to the right. Between the grevillea and the lowest fern add three stems of grasses and more, with their graceful raindrop effect, near the tallest grass. Over the front rim of the container and towards the back on the

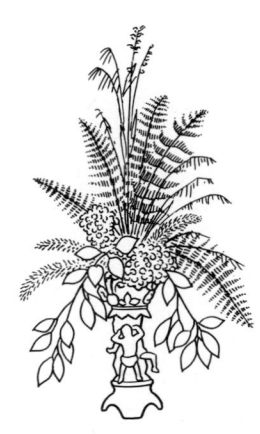

left add two short stems of bright yellow-green euphorbia flower heads.

2 Use spray carnations to accentuate the outline, down below the beech on the right, in front of it on the left, up by the grass and then follow the lines of the ferns, finishing with a spray in front of the beech on the left. Add the dicentra stems, forward and down on the right, and then place stems of alstroemerias towards the middle of the arrangement.

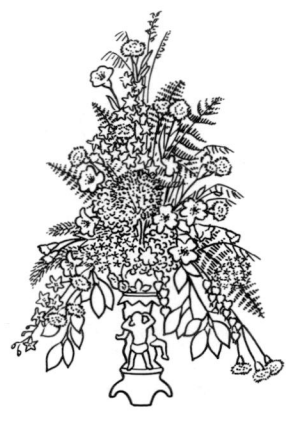

3 Add the orchids and the alliums next. Put the orchids in a line down the middle and out, low, on the left. Place one of the two greyish flowers of *Allium karataviense* on the left, just over the rim; the other should go on the right, over the dicentra but within the original outline, shorter than the fern. Add the purple allium head below the spray of orchids in the middle. Three roses and two large-flowered carnations complete the arrangement. Group the roses to the right of and below the last allium. Put one carnation between the two stems of dicentra and another on the left between the ferns and the larch.

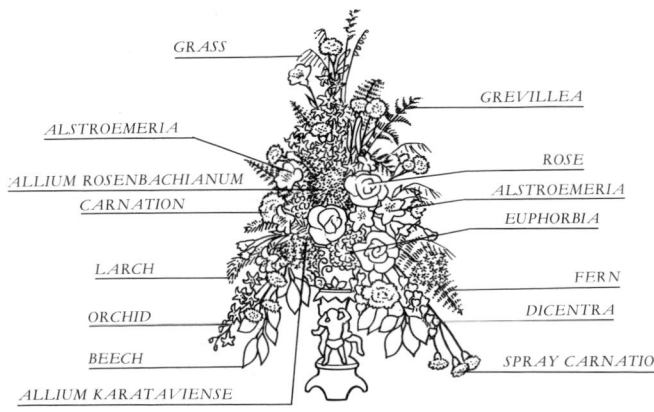

GRASS

GREVILLEA

ALSTROEMERIA

ROSE

ALLIUM ROSENBACHIANUM

ALSTROEMERIA

CARNATION

EUPHORBIA

LARCH

FERN

ORCHID

DICENTRA

BEECH

SPRAY CARNATIONS

ALLIUM KARATAVIENSE

4 Place the two shells just to the right of the cherub. Fill one with pot-pourri. Once more, the colours in the background are picked up.

THE 'STILL LIFE' by
Pieter de Ring is dated 1660 and
is a fine example of his work. To
assemble a group in the same mood is
tempting, even a personal indulgence,
but doing so tells the arranger a great
deal about the painting and the result is
suitable for a very special occasion.
Here the flowers and fruits of high
summer pay tribute to the artist.

SIZE
145 cm × 89 cm × 63½ cm
(57 in × 35 in × 25 in).

CONTAINERS
A basket 25½ cm (10 in) in diameter, with a
round dish inside, 18 cm (7 in) in diameter.
A plastic dish, 18 cm (7 in) in diameter.
A round dish, 10 cm (4 in) in diameter,
2½ cm (1 in) deep.

EQUIPMENT
Blocks of well-soaked foam, cut to fit each
container and taped across. Blocks of wood:
5 cm × 15 cm × 15 cm (2 in × 6 in × 6 in)
(one); 10 cm × 10 cm × 10 cm
(4 in × 4 in × 4 in) (two);
23 cm × 15 cm × 15 cm (9 in × 6 in × 6 in)
(one); 2½ cm × 10 cm × 10 cm
(1 in × 4 in × 4 in) (one). Two plate stands.

FOLIAGE
Cynara cardunculus (cardoon).
Vitis vinifera 'Incana' (dusty miller
grape).
Vitis vinifera (wine grape).

FLOWERS
Delphiniums.
Lilium martagon (martagon lily).
Papaver somniferum 'Peony-flowered'
(double flowered opium poppy).
Lilium 'Sun kissed' (lily) (tiger lily).
Lonicera periclymenum 'Serotina' (late
Dutch honeysuckle, woodbine).
Iris, bearded hybrid 'Grace Sturtevant'
(German iris).
Campanula persicifolia (*C. grandis, C.*
latiloba) (willow bellflower).
Rose 'Fragrant Cloud'.
Papaver orientale 'Turkish Delight'
(oriental poppy).
Rose 'Blessings'.
Paeonia lactiflora 'Sarah Bernhardt'
(double peony).

FRUIT
A stem of gooseberries, one orange, one
peach, three pears, two apples, two lemons,
bunches of grapes (green, black and brown),
one nectarine, one small orange-fleshed melon
and 'White Heart' cherries.

DUTCH SCHOOL

ACCESSORIES
Two pieces of velvet, 1½ metres
in a sea green colour and ½
metre in turquoise. A silk
cord and tassle in coral-red.
Two bronze ewers, two pewter
plates, one tazza base, one
brass alms dish, one blue Delft
plate, one glass carafe, one
wine glass and one artificial
lobster.

ARRANGER
Norah Phillippo

1 Set up the acces-
sories, starting with
the blocks of wood (see
diagram). With the larger
piece of velvet cover these
blocks and drape the
material across from the
back right-hand corner of
the chest to fall over the
front edge towards the left.
Use the bright turquoise
piece on the left. Place the
tassle to come forward
over the edge of the chest,
just to the right of the
centre, taking the cord
back and then to the left,
looping it forward again
over the edge in front of
the block on the left-hand
side. Place the basket on
the lowest piece of wood,
the ewers on the two
blocks to the right of it and
the plastic container on the
block on the far right. In
front of this dish stand the
brass alms dish, angled
towards the left but
screening the dish from the
front view. Next to it stand
the tazza base, then rest the
Delft plate behind but
propped up against the
velvet-covered block. This
plate should be turned
towards the left. Put the
lobster half on the plate

and over the cord and on a
small pewter plate. This
plate should be nearly in
the middle and at the front
of the chest. Leave some
space before placing the
larger of the two pewter
plates against its stand on
the left, towards the back;
turn this plate slightly to
the right. To the right of
this plate stand the glass
and in front of it, on the
block, place the half-full
decanter. The scene is set
for the flowers.

2 Add delphiniums on
the right; arrange them
with the martagon lilies in
the container hidden
behind the brass alms dish.
Give depth behind the
delphiniums, on their right,
with one of the three grey
cardoon leaves. Add a
second in front of the
flowers and a third a little
lower and out behind the
dish, both curving to the
right. The lilies should be
placed together, near the
tallest delphinium. A small
leaf of cardoon curved
round behind the dish will
hide the foam and the
container from the right
but should not be seen
from the front. In the
basket, arrange the double
crimson poppies and tiger
lilies. Place the tallest lily at
the back. Take the lowest
stem of lilies to the left.

Place the smallest container behind the decanter; the cord should mask the front. Place a stem of gooseberries from this container to come towards the right and out over the edge of the chest. Add two stems of honeysuckle, one over the cord and the other towards the wall.

3 Complete both of the larger groups by adding two bearded iris in front of the delphiniums and lilies. Add a few pale blue campanulas to the second group and two 'Fragrant Cloud' roses, one near the top on the left, the other nearer the centre. Add the peony, just to the left of the centre, a fully open, flesh-pink poppy above but to the right, a second poppy low down on the right and a 'Blessings' rose to its left at the front. Take two stems of vine, leaves and tendrils, and bring them from this group, one low down on

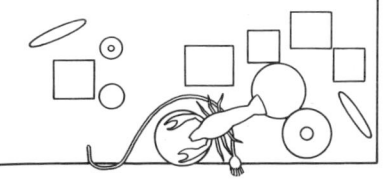

the right and another, from the middle, to come just above the lower of the two single poppy flowers.

4 Add the fruit, starting at the chest level. Group green, black and brown grapes from the brass plate towards the right, oranges and a lemon behind. Add an apple next in front of the vine, and peaches by the lobster's claw. From the left, start with green grapes, two apples and the melon, a slice cut out and resting on the front apple. Add a further apple behind the pewter plate. On top of the tazza put a pear, some cherries and a half-peeled

lemon, the rind falling down towards the chest. Add a few more cherries beside the black grapes. Above, on the tallest block, in front of the ewer, add two more pears and a small bunch of green grapes.

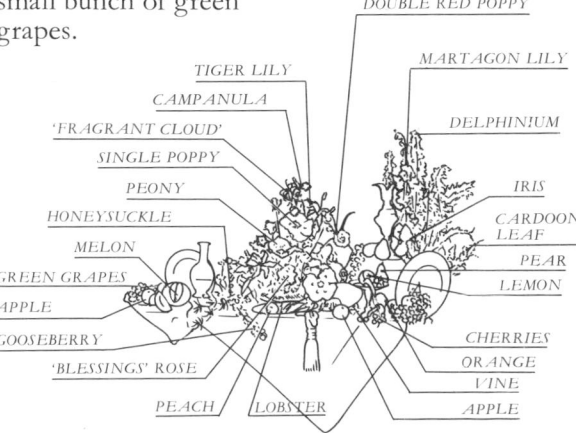

DOUBLE RED POPPY
TIGER LILY
MARTAGON LILY
CAMPANULA
'FRAGRANT CLOUD'
DELPHINIUM
SINGLE POPPY
PEONY
IRIS
HONEYSUCKLE
CARDOON LEAF
MELON
PEAR
GREEN GRAPES
LEMON
APPLE
GOOSEBERRY
'BLESSINGS' ROSE
CHERRIES
ORANGE
VINE
PEACH
LOBSTER
APPLE

MID-SUMMER'S DAY

PERFUME AND colour from the garden fills this fire-place. The ferns in the background contrast delightfully with the full petalled flowers and the stately spires of delphiniums.

SIZE
91½ cm × 107 cm (36 in × 42 in).

CONTAINER
A round metal bowl on small feet, 25½ cm × 10 cm (10 in × 4 in).

EQUIPMENT
Three blocks of foam, well soaked, two towards the back and one, centrally, in the front, standing 15 cm (6 in) above the rim.

FOLIAGE
Athyrium felix-femina (lady fern).

FLOWERS
Viburnum × carlcephalum (fragrant snowball).
Philadelphus coronarius (mock orange).
Delphiniums.
Paeonia lactiflora 'Lady Alexandra Duff', pale pink, and P.l. 'M. Jules Elle', darker pink (peony).

ARRANGER
Evelyn Mercer

1 The ferns are used to give a tracery effect at the back and sides of the arrangement. Place them in a triangular shape which is low on the left with a frond taken out over the inner part of the fireplace. From the centre top arrange fronds coming forward and down, finishing half-way between the centre front and the right-hand side. Add the viburnum next, a stem by the fern on the left, one towards the back on the right and two more, low in the arrangement, then a full-flowered stem on the right and a slender stem coming forward over the hearth in the front.

2 Fill in the lower part of the arrangement with the stems of philadelphus, remembering to take off most of the leaves first or the flowers will fade very quickly. Add a delphinium in the middle, just in front of the tallest fern, and then use the six peonies, three very pale pink and three darker pink. Place a darker one in front of the delphinium with two of the paler ones below and at either side of it. Place the third pale one lower again on the right. The two remaining flowers are the darker pink. Place the first of these in the middle of the design and the other to its right but a little lower.

3 Complete the arrangement by adding the delphiniums, some among the peonies and one out to the left. Then, with two shorter stems, add more blue to the design, just higher than the hearth, one stem coming forward in the middle and the second turned a little to the right.

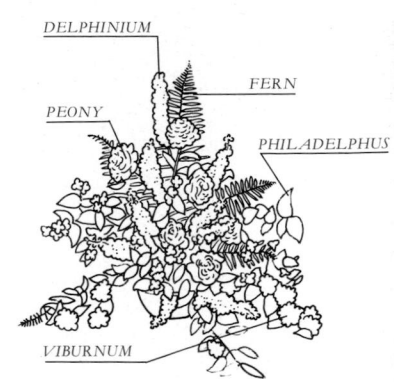

DELPHINIUM

FERN

PEONY

PHILADELPHUS

VIBURNUM

A TRADITIONAL mass arrangement with flowing lines, bold enough to have impact in its grand setting and complementing but not competing with the architectural detail.

Colours of rich orange, crimson, gold, brown and purple reflect in the copper, link it with the gilt picture frame and take full advantage of the attractive blue-green wall behind and the white plasterwork of the wall panel.

SIZE
105 cm × 75 cm (42 in × 30 in).

CONTAINER
An antique copper urn of the Adam period. Long, elegant handles and a circular lid. 42 cm × 35 cm (17 in × 14 in). The lid is 23 cm (9 in) in diameter. An antique Sheffield plate gallery tray is used as a base.

EQUIPMENT
A shallow metal dish is fitted to the top of the urn by attaching it carefully to the handles. A square of foam, standing 7 cm (3 in) above the rim of the dish, is covered with wire netting and this, too, is attached carefully to the handles with soft twine.

FOLIAGE
Hosta sieboldiana (plantain lily).
Vitis coignetiae (Japanese crimson glory vine).

FLOWERS
Red gladioli.
Cluster roses (Floribundas) 'Iced Ginger' and 'Sweet Repose'.
Red and orange dahlias, both decorative and water-lily types.

OTHER PLANT MATERIAL
Atriplex hortensis 'Rubra' (orache, mountain spinach) with its seed-heads.
Physalis franchetii (Cape gooseberry, Chinese lanterns).
Lathyrus latifolius (everlasting pea) seed-heads.
Rosa rubrifolia with its crimson hips. Worcester Permain apples, Conference pears, Victoria plums, cob-nuts, horse chestnuts (conkers) and *Vitis vinifera* 'Purpurea' (garden wall grapes).

ARRANGER
Norah Phillippo

THE WARM GLOW OF COPPER

1 Form the outline using five stems of mountain spinach, five of Chinese lanterns, three of everlasting pea seed-heads and *Rosa rubrifolia* stems. Then place three large hosta leaves, just turning to their golden autumn colour, in the centre and angle two richly coloured purple vine leaves one from the left and slightly forward, the other out and down to the front right.

2 Use the gladioli to strengthen the outline and roses and dahlias to give importance to the centre of the design. These can all follow the already established lines.

3 More roses and dahlias emphasize the colour groupings. Place the urn on the tray with the lid set at an angle on the right and slightly behind the urn. The fruit is grouped from right to left, overflowing onto the marble top of the imposing side table.

MOUNTAIN SPINACH
GLADIOLUS
CHINESE LANTERNS
HOSTA
EVERLASTING PEA
DAHLIA

ROSE

VINE LEAF

ROSA RUBRIFOLIA

AUTUMN BOUNTY

HANDSOME CARVED marble and polished steel make an imposing setting for flowers and a bold design of rich colours is needed to create a grand effect. The arrangement is raised from the hearth level by using a stemmed container and this leaves the pattern of the fender showing clearly and gives a more pleasing effect than if a low container had been used.

Crimson, scarlet, apricot, brown and light green are the colours mixed together in this arrangement. They glow warmly against the background of steel and marble.

SIZE
124 cm × 100 cm (50 in × 40 in).

CONTAINER
Two tiers of an alabaster compote
35 cm × 20 cm (14 in × 8 in) wide at the top.

EQUIPMENT
After lining the alabaster bowl to avoid damage from water, half a block of foam, placed in a plastic dish and covered with wire netting, is attached carefully to the container with tape.

FOLIAGE
Hedera helix 'Glacier' (variegated ivy).
Paeonia lactiflora (peony).

FLOWERS
Gladioli.
Various fuchsias.
Vallota speciosa (Scarborough lily).
Florists' spray chrysanthemums.
Cactus dahlia 'Preference'.
Red florists' roses 'Baccarat'.

OTHER PLANT MATERIAL
Humulus lupulus 'Aureus' (golden hop).
Seed-heads of *Clematis tangutica.*
Malus 'John Downie' crab apples.

ARRANGER
José Allen

1 Establish the necessary height for this large arrangement with the tallest stem of gladiolus. Two slightly shorter stems, one behind and one just to the left, give support to this line. Use graceful stems of fuchsias and variegated ivy for width. Place brown peony leaves in the centre to give depth to the design. Add more flowing lines with a few pieces of ivy.

2 Place the beautiful and brilliant Scarborough lily in front of the dark peony leaves and take the apricot-coloured chrysanthemums towards the back to show up against the steel. The 'Preference' dahlias add highlights among the darker colours.

3 Add more dahlias and thread red roses through the centre; these are also used in profile at the outside of the design. Finally, add golden hop, clematis seed-heads and crab apples, which trail over the fender, to suggest the abundance of the season.

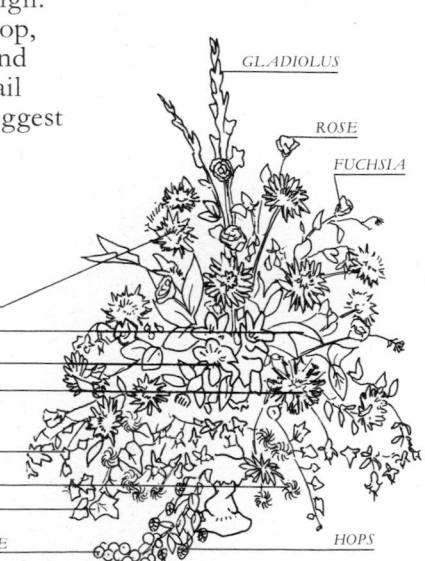

GLADIOLUS
ROSE
FUCHSIA
CHRYSANTHEMUM
PEONY LEAVES
SCARBOROUGH LILY
DAHLIA
STEPHANANDRA
CLEMATIS SEED HEADS
IVY
CRAB APPLE
HOPS

EDWARDIAN ELEGANCE

AN INFORMAL flowing and airy arrangement, based on a triangular design. This is chosen to echo the furnishings. The little table is elegant with gentle curves and these are repeated in the way the material is used above the bed.

The pink, grey and white of the flowers and foliage repeat the colours in the room and the china on the table.

SIZE
68 cm × 45 cm (27 in × 18 in).

CONTAINER
A china shell with scalloped edge held aloft by three dolphins, white, 25 cm (10 in) tall.

EQUIPMENT
Well soaked foam and wire netting to cover.

FOLIAGE
Eucalyptus gunnii (gum tree) and Chrysanthemum haradjanii (Tanacetum densum amani) (both grey).

FLOWERS
Nicotiana alata (tobacco plant) in soft dark red.
Lilium speciosum 'Melpomene', a lily with crimson spots on white petals and with elegant buds; this is a late flowering lily.
Florists' pink spray carnations.

OTHER PLANT MATERIAL
Fruiting sprays of *Symphoricarpus albus* 'Laevitagus' (snowberry).

ACCESSORIES
Delicate small china dish and jug on its own stand.

ARRANGER
Marjorie Watling

1 Half a block of foam is covered with a fairly loose layer of wire-netting which is carefully fastened to the container in three places. The outline of the design is formed with three sprays of eucalyptus.

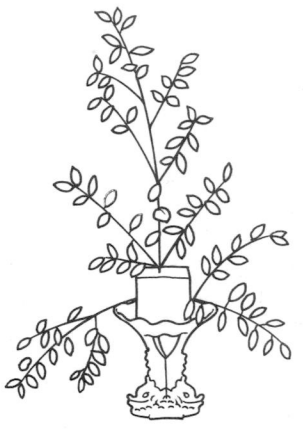

3 Grey foliage, the feathery chrysanthemum, is used in the heart of the arrangement and sprays of snowberry emphasize the outline at the front, flowing out to soften the edge of the container.

2 The stems of the lilies are placed to follow the outline, the buds being as important as the open flowers. The tobacco plant flowers are taken through the middle of the design to give some depth of colour there.

4 Spray carnations are used sparingly to fill in the design and a few more tobacco plant flowers are placed towards the back to stop the design merging with the soft colour of the wall.

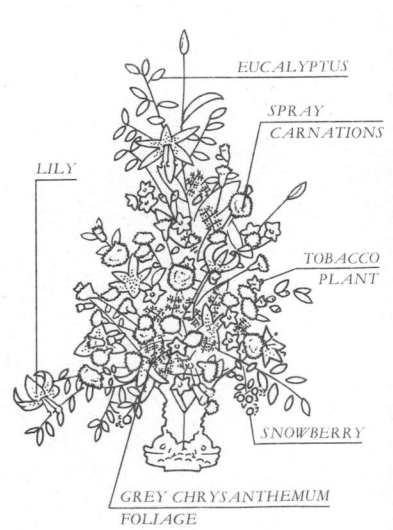

EUCALYPTUS
SPRAY CARNATIONS
LILY
TOBACCO PLANT
SNOWBERRY
GREY CHRYSANTHEMUM FOLIAGE

TEXTURES

IN THIS elegant drawing room the marquetry table is painted with *trompe l'oeil* cards, coins and documents. It stands below a landscape painting and the arrangement echoes some of the soft colours in it and the detail of the table.

Grey, gold, crimson, lemon-yellow and green, from very dark to soft grey-green, are blended together. The textures too, are varied.

SIZE
91 cm × 40 cm (36 in × 16 in).

CONTAINER
An oval, silver-plated cruet-stand, 18 cm × 14 cm (7 in × 5½ in) at the widest parts, on feet and standing 8 cm (3 in) high. Two oval bases, each 2 cm (¾ in) thick, covered in 'old gold' velvet, are placed below the container. The larger is 41 cm (16 in) and the smaller 26 cm (10 in) across.

EQUIPMENT
A bowl, used as a liner, has a square of well-soaked foam which comes above the rim a further 8 cm (3 in).

FOLIAGE
Onopordum acanthium (cotton or Scotch thistle).
Stephanandra incisa 'Crispa' *(s.i. prostrata).*

FLOWERS
Fuchsia magellanica 'Gracilis Variegata'.
Fuchsia fulgens.
Achillea taygetea (yarrow).

OTHER PLANT MATERIAL
Pyracantha rogersiana 'Flava' (firethorn).

ARRANGER
Marjorie Watling

1 Place the container centrally on the two bases which are placed on top of each other. The pyracantha makes an interesting outline. The tallest stem is positioned first, coming from just behind the centre of the foam, but off-centre to the right at its top. Balance this with a heavily berried stem low to the left with a shorter piece a little nearer to the centre but still angled to the left. On the right use a further but less weighty stem to come slightly forward and a fifth behind it but going out towards the wall. The design is visually balanced by the careful placing of these heavy stems. Add the variegated fuchsia, with red flowers and grey-green foliage, to provide brighter highlights.

2 Grey onopordum leaves are used to form a background for the *Fuchsia fulgens* flowers and, sprays of elegant stephanandra foliage follow the same lines.

3 Thread pale lemon-yellow flowers of the small-growing achillea through in a diagonal line from right to left. These emphasize the design and pick up the colour of the bases, giving another change of texture.

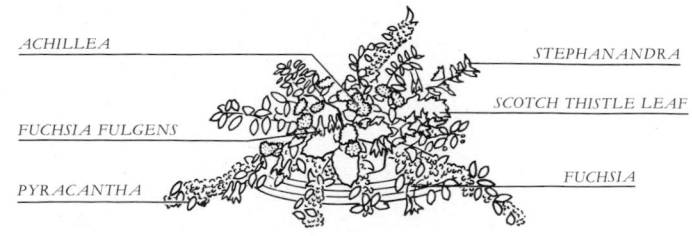

ACHILLEA
STEPHANANDRA
SCOTCH THISTLE LEAF
FUCHSIA FULGENS
FUCHSIA
PYRACANTHA

REFLECTIONS

A DELICATE and informal posy which harmonizes beautifully with its setting. The arrangement appears to fall quite naturally, and no mechanics show to spoil the charm of the delicate glass vase. The arrangement is reflected in the mirror from many angles.

Cream, apricot, crimson and blue-grey are the colours which form links with the soft pink of the vase, the picture and the mirror's beautiful gilt frame.

SIZE
32 cm × 20 cm (13 in × 8 in).

CONTAINER
Delicate stemmed glass vase with applied glass decoration. The glass is colourless in the middle and shades down to pink in the stem and foot, and up to its rim. 12 cm × 9 cm (6 in × 3½ in).

EQUIPMENT
A 12 cm (5 in). long plant tie (covered wire).

FOLIAGE
Ruta graveolens 'Jackman's Blue' (rue).

FLOWERS
Florists' rose 'Champagne'.
Alstroemeria 'Ligtu Hybrids' (Peruvian lily).
Florists' spray chrysanthemum 'Apricot Marble'.
Fuchsia magellanica 'Riccartonii'.

OTHER PLANT MATERIAL
Symphoricarpos albus (common snowberry) berries.

ARRANGER
Felicity Bickley

1 Place the water-filled vase in front of the mirror and to one side. Arrange the posy in your hand, making sure there is a natural flow to the stems and that there is all round interest. Hold it fairly loosely until it is complete. Use the soft cream roses and alstroemeria from the top down to the middle and rue and chrysanthemums in the middle. All should be used sparingly and with any surplus leaves removed.

2 Fuchsia and snow-berries are added last to fall gracefully to the sides and over the rim of the vase.

3 Take the plant tie round the bunch and fit it firmly at the level which will be below the rim of the vase and will not be seen. The posy is placed in the vase and, if necessary, the vase is turned, to make sure all the reflected views are as pleasing as that seen from the front.

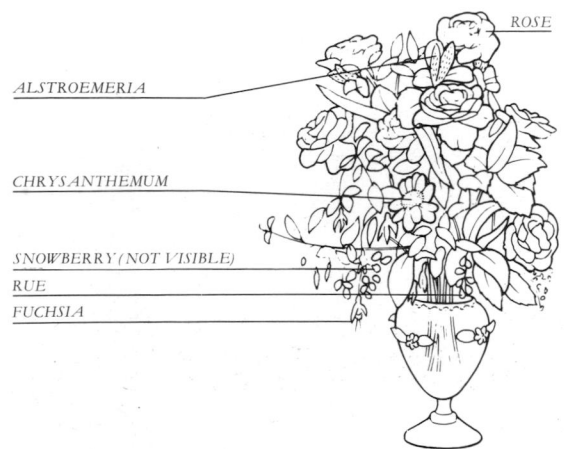

ROSE

ALSTROEMERIA

CHRYSANTHEMUM

SNOWBERRY (NOT VISIBLE)
RUE
FUCHSIA

A FINE selection of foliage picked on a dreary winter day stands on a low table in front of a large picture window with the curtains pulled across behind the arrangement. It brings the garden indoors for the evening just as the window allows it to be enjoyed during daylight hours.

Among the many shades of green there are yellows, soft red and bronze. The lines of colour in the phormium leaves are in harmony with the faint shadow stripes and the folds in the curtains.

SIZE
114 cm × 125 cm (45 in × 49 in).

CONTAINER
A metal bowl, 20 cm × 5 cm (8 in × 2 in).
A carved wooden stand, 23 cm (9 in) across its base, 13 cm (5 in) high.

EQUIPMENT
Two large pieces of foam, one fitting across the bowl at the front, the other standing on end 15 cm (6 in) above the rim. Both pieces fit firmly and are taped to the bowl.

FOLIAGE
Phormiums (New Zealand flax):
Phormium tenax 'Veitchii; *P.t.* 'Sundowner'; *P.t.* 'Thumbelina'; *P. cookianum* 'Aurora'.
Prunus lusitanica 'Variegata' (Portugal laurel).
Camellia japonica.
Leucothoe catesbaei 'Rainbow'.
Hypericum calycinum (St. John's wort, Aaron's beard, rose of Sharon).
Hedera helix 'Glacier' and *H. canariensis* (ivies).
Rhamnus alaternus 'Argenteovariegata' (buckthorn).
Fatsia japonica (aralia).
Grevillea robusta (silk oak) from the greenhouse.
Eucalyptus mitchelliana (gum tree, weeping sally).
Helichrysum angustifolium (curry plant).
Elaeagnus pungens 'Gold Edge'.
Rhododendron obovata.

ARRANGER
Pamela McNicol

LEAVES FROM A WINTER GARDEN

1 Group the different types of phormium leaves together first, creating a strong but elegant line and variety of colour in the centre of the design at the back. Two of the leaves on the right are bent over carefully and the tips anchored in the foam. Bring elaeagnus, camellia foliage and a stem of leucothoe from behind and towards the sides of the phormiums. At the front, with trails of both ivies, a stem of leucothoe on the right and one of hypericum on the left establish the width of the arrangement to come forward over the edge of the table. Place two pieces of buckthorn near the centre.

2 Build up the design within this outline, carefully avoiding filling it out into a complete half circle. Use fatsia and grevillea to strengthen the design at the sides, also prunus and more of the camellia. These are balanced on the left with a third piece of leucothoe, a graceful piece of eucalyptus and a stem of the grey, spiky textured curry plant. Another stem of eucalyptus will soften the starkness of the phormium leaves and place a third behind the leucothoe on the right. Use the elaeagnus on either side of and behind the phormium grouping.

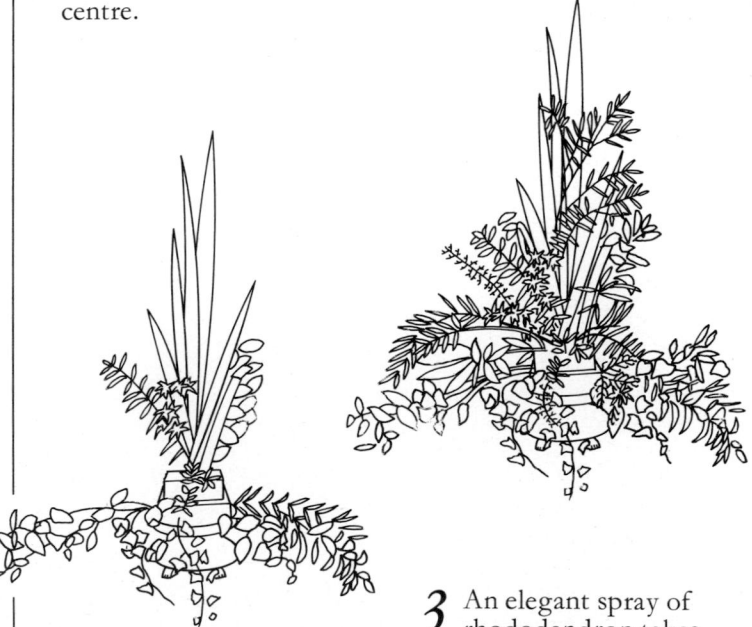

3 An elegant spray of rhododendron takes pride of place in the centre. Cut it so that the branch

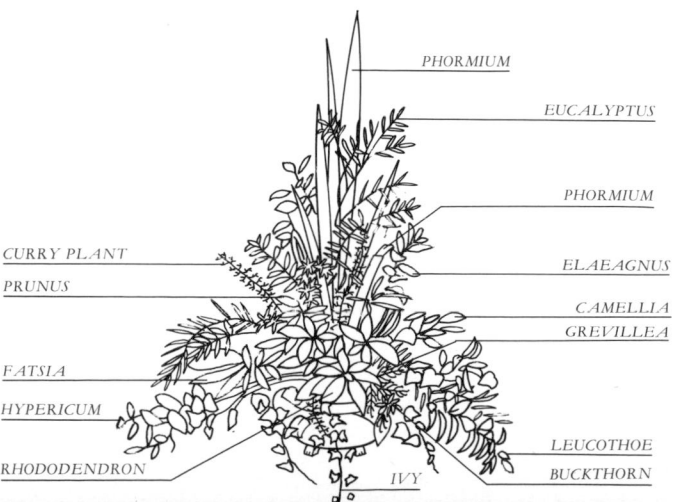

can be placed in the foam
to come forward naturally
and so show off the
beautiful variegation. Place
a little more of the curry
plant just above it. Shorter
pieces of various foliages,
used towards and at the
back, will cover the foam
but not confuse the
finished design.

PHORMIUM

EUCALYPTUS

PHORMIUM

CURRY PLANT

PRUNUS

ELAEAGNUS

CAMELLIA

GREVILLEA

FATSIA

HYPERICUM

RHODODENDRON

IVY

LEUCOTHOE

BUCKTHORN

57

THERE IS a timeless quality in the oak panelling, the 17th century chair and the subtle colours of the needlework picture and this has been picked up with the dried flowers, foliage and seed-heads used in the arrangement on the sofa table.

Red rosebuds and a velvet base echo the soft dark red in the picture and the china, while neutral colours are used to form the outline and to create a background, just as they do in the room itself and in the embroidery.

SIZE
78 cm × 47 cm (30½ in × 18½ in).

CONTAINER
A black bowl, 15 cm (6 in) in diameter. A velvet covered red base, oval, 51 cm × 32 cm (20 in × 12½ in).

EQUIPMENT
A square of dry foam, cut to fit across the bowl, standing 4 cm (1½ in) above the rim.

FOLIAGE
Fagus sylvatica (common beech), glycerined.
Skeletonized magnolia leaves, dyed red (purchased).

FLOWERS
Artemisia absinthium (common wormwood), air dried.
Pink and red rosebuds with their leaves, freeze dried (purchased).
Blue salvia (sage) (purchased).
Gypsophila paniculata (baby's breath, chalk plant), air dried and dyed red.

OTHER PLANT MATERIAL
Ballota acetabulosa (horehound), air-dried stems with bracts.
Nigella damascena seedheads (love-in-a-mist, devil-in-the-bush) air dried.
Papaver somniferum (poppy) seedheads air dried.

ACCESSORIES
A silver candlestick with a soft-blue candle, a coffee cup and a little posy.

ARRANGER
Pearl Frost

OAK PARLOUR

1 Take the stems of parchment-coloured ballota and the more slender, grey artemisia to form the outline, the tallest piece being approximately the same height as the red base is wide. Both the longest outside stems are also about this length. Depth of form and colour is added with the sprays of beech in the centre.

2 Next take the delicate looking magnolia leaves and place them among the contrasting beech leaves. Use the striped seedheads of the nigella towards the outside of the design with just a few nearer the centre.

3 Follow the triangular shape by adding the pink rosebuds and the poppy seedheads, a little nearer the centre than the nigella, and then add a few sprays of the gypsophila flowers to introduce dark red at the sides and towards the front on the right.

4 Richness is added with the blue salvias and the dark red rosebuds. Use some of the salvias at either side and in the centre and then take the rosebuds, bringing them through the design, recessing some and bringing others forward to avoid a flat effect when the arrangement is finished. The top rose should be just below the tallest stem of ballota and the lowest brought forward at the front just above the base. Add the pale blue candle to complete the colour links between the picture and the arrangement.

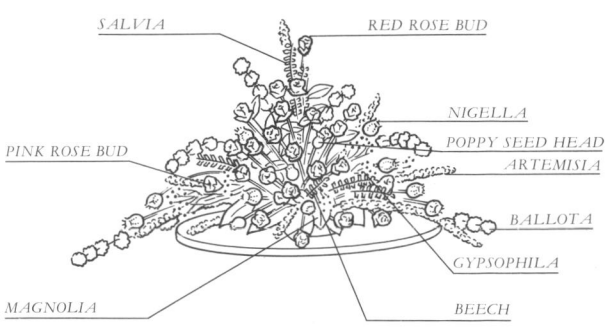

SALVIA   RED ROSE BUD

NIGELLA

POPPY SEED HEAD

PINK ROSE BUD   ARTEMISIA

BALLOTA

GYPSOPHILA

MAGNOLIA   BEECH

CHRISTMAS MORNING

STANDING IN the ingle-nook, behind the massive oak beam, is an arrangement on a low pedestal. The patterns of the brickwork, the iron fire-basket, screen and fire-irons and the hinged pot-holder make a fascinating setting from the past.

Fresh evergreens with terracotta-coloured flowers pick up the colours in the bricks and a few golden baubles add a festive 20th century sparkle. The parcels on the hearth are wrapped in paper which repeats the golden gleam of the baubles.

SIZE
140 cm × 104 cm (55 in × 41 in).

CONTAINER
A small wrought-iron pedestal with its own bowl container, 66 cm (26 in) high (plus the bowl), 8 cm (3 in) deep and 25 cm (10 in) across its base.

EQUIPMENT
Two blocks of foam, securely fixed with tape.

FOLIAGE
Eucalyptus mitchelliana (gum tree, weeping sally).
Hedera canariensis 'Variegata' ('Gloire de Marengo') (Canary Island ivy).
Camellia Elaeagnus pungens 'Limelight'.
Euonymus fortunei radicans 'Emerald Gaiety' (spindle).
Ilex aquifolium 'Golden Queen' ('Aurea Regina') (English holly).
Rhododendron obovata.

FLOWERS
Single spray chrysanthemums.

OTHER PLANT MATERIAL
Heavily berried *Ilex aquifolium* 'Bacciflava' (yellow-fruited holly).

ACCESSORIES
Gold baubles mounted on long stub wires, these covered in green stem tape.

ARRANGER
Pamela McNicol

1 Create a flowing outline with the dainty eucalyptus foliage at the top and to the sides, the larger scale variegated ivy on the right-hand side and down at the front and the bold leaves of elaeagnus and camellia to the left behind the fire-screen. Place three stems of the yellow-berried holly, one centrally at the top, one down to the left towards the screen and the third out to the right and slightly forward. A stem of the variegated euonymus is used near the holly at the front.

2 Place the variegated holly at the centre front and towards the back on both sides. Now add long stems of spray chrysanthemums informally throughout the design. A stem of the unusual variegated rhododendron is placed on the left above the camellia.

3 As a final touch the gold baubles are placed to follow the central triangular pattern. Because they are on long stems they will fall quite gracefully and catch the light, as do the foil-wrapped presents with their dark green velvet ribbons and sprigs of the berried holly.

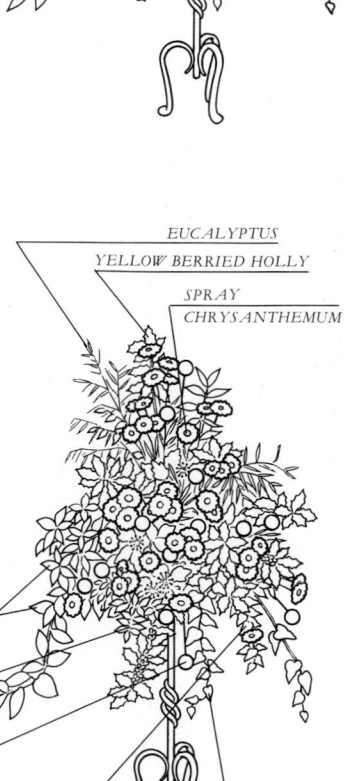

EUCALYPTUS
YELLOW BERRIED HOLLY
SPRAY CHRYSANTHEMUM
CAMELLIA
VARIEGATED RHODODENDRON
EUONYMUS
ELAEAGNUS
GOLD BAUBLE
VARIEGATED HOLLY
IVY

YULETIDE

THROUGH THE centuries this lovely Tudor home has seen the Christmas season come and go. The ancient timbers frame a carved and gilded *torchère* of a later date and this holds aloft an arrangement of flowers for today's Christmas celebrations. Placed at the turn of the stairs it has been designed to look attractive from both above and below the viewer and also to be quite slim so that it does not take up too much room as people pass.

The traditional colours of rich red and shining dark green are enlivened with the sparkle of glittered 'fern'.

SIZE
200 cm × 76 cm (79 in × 30 in).

CONTAINER
A torchère, 92 cm (36 in) high, holding a large round pottery bowl, 25 cm (10 in) in diameter.

EQUIPMENT
One whole and one half block of foam, the larger used on end at the back of the bowl with the half block in front, both taped across the bowl firmly.

FOLIAGE
Ilex aquifolium (English or common holly) and *I.a.* 'Silver Queen'.
Picea glauca (white or Canadian spruce).
Hedera canariensis (Canary Island ivy).
Skimmia japonica.

FLOWERS
Spray and large carnations, gladioli and roses 'Mercedes', all from the florist.
Euphorbia pulcherrima (poinsettia) with the stem ends singed as soon as cut from the plants.

ACCESSORIES
Red glittered artificial 'fern' and 2½ metres of red flock ribbon.

ARRANGER
Pearl Frost

1 Use the curving pieces of both kinds of holly first to give the outline. Turn the top piece of holly slightly to the left and turn the two lowest pieces, on both sides, in towards the figure. Those just above follow the same line but not quite so dramatically. Add a few shorter pieces of holly up through the middle of the arrangement. Next add the spruce, three sprays, one to come forward and down at the front over the edge of the bowl, the others further back and low down on either side. Place large ivy leaves in the middle to give a dark background for the flowers and to mask the foam and then, to add a lighter green, use two stems of skimmia above the ivy.

2 Use both the spray and the large red carnations in flowing lines on either side of the arrangement and three stems of scarlet gladioli in the middle to add a strong line of colour.

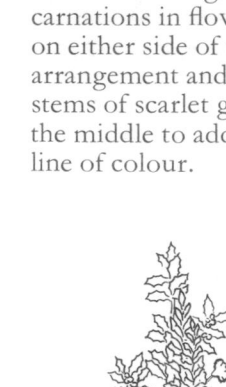

3 Now fill the centre of the design without making it too bulky. Take the sparkling 'fern' and curve it a little so that it has more graceful lines, then use some in profile and some to show more obviously, repeating the triangular shape of the outline. Seven sprays are needed. The velvety textured poinsettias come next and each stem is used where it will play an important part in the design. The stem ends, having been burnt to seal them, must be put in individual small tubes of water and these tubes fixed in the foam with care to avoid splitting it unnecessarily. The tallest poinsettia goes up with the gladioli, then one on the right, to be seen to advantage when coming down the stairs, and one on the left to balance the design when it is viewed from below. Place the fourth stem a little to the left and above the centre and the fifth one low down on the right. The remaining space between these last two blooms is for the ribbon bow. Make it with a flat double loop and add four trailers, two long and two much shorter. Wire each piece separately and then fix them in the foam so that the finished effect is of one generous, tailored bow.

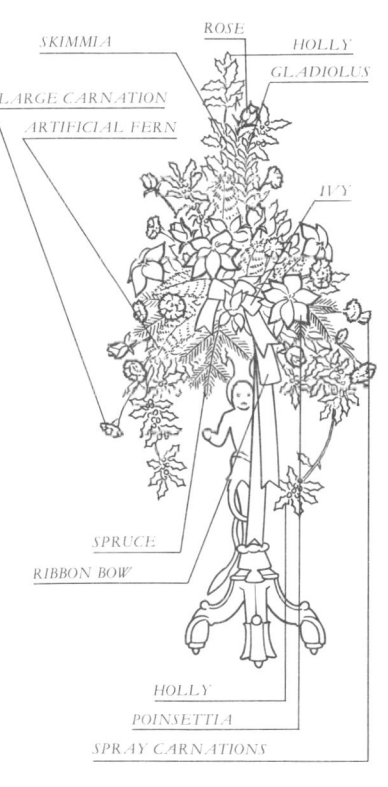

SKIMMIA
ROSE
HOLLY
GLADIOLUS
LARGE CARNATION
ARTIFICIAL FERN
IVY
SPRUCE
RIBBON BOW
HOLLY
POINSETTIA
SPRAY CARNATIONS

LONG-LASTING plant material is used in this modern arrangement which successfully draws attention to its 19th century setting. The flowers and the phormium leaves are, like their background, richly red and brown and, although the arrangement is tall it does not appear unduly so with the staircase rising and turning around it.

The bold loops of the phormium leaves are important to the balance of the design. Without them the palm leaf on the left, with its strong shape and colour, would be too heavy and the way the loops are placed adds depth and movement to the arrangement. Pointed leaf tips used in place of loops would have been dramatic but would have appeared static.

SIZE
127 cm × 40 cm (50 in × 15¾ in).

CONTAINERS
A hand-thrown pottery vase, cylindrical in shape, 30 cm × 19 cm (11¾ in × 7½ in), on three wooden stands, the top one upside-down. Both top and bottom stands are carved, the middle one is plain, 12 cm (4¾ in) high in all. A well pinholder, 6 cm (2¼ in) in diameter, standing on another carved wooden stand, 9 cm (3½ in) in diameter.

EQUIPMENT
Sand in the pottery container to within 7½ cm (3 in) of the top and a heavy pinholder 12½ cm (5 in) in diameter placed on top of the level sand.

FOLIAGE
Phormium tenax 'Purpureum' (New Zealand flax), fresh leaves.
Chamaerops humilis (European fan palm), fresh leaves.
Phoenix canariensis (Canary date palm), a dried leaf.

FLOWERS
Anthurium scherzerianum (flamingo flower).

ARRANGER
Peggy Crooks

FLAMINGO FLOWERS AND FLAX

1 The tall phormium leaves are put in position first. Place one leaf centrally on the pinholder in the pottery container, then two more, both curved and taped in position, forming loops. Place the taller loop on the pinholder slightly behind and to the right of the first leaf and turn it halfway towards the back of the container. The stem of the second loop should be shorter. Place this stem in front of the first leaf and

2 Trim two small sections of the green palm into sharply triangular shapes and place these stems in the middle of the well pinholder, the one on the right a little taller than the other. This pinholder is placed on its stand just to the left of the other stands. Take them up, together, in a straight line just to the left of the pottery container.

In front of the back two phormium leaves, place the dried date palm leaf, its top coming just higher than the top phormium loop and directly under the tip of the first leaf. In front of this dried leaf, and to its left, place a fan of the fresh palm, again trimmed,

turn it towards the front, again about halfway.

cutting off all discoloured and damaged tips and forming an even curve round three-quarters of a circle. Put this leaf on the pinholder so that it curves round from in front of the date palm and down, finishing in the centre again directly under the tip of the first phormium.

3 Add the anthuriums;
form a diagonal line
with five stems across the
arrangement, from the left
down to the right,
staggering the placing and
turning the spathes a little
to avoid a flat effect. Put
the sixth anthurium in the
front of the well pinholder,
just above the carpet and
turning to the left and the
foot of the stairs.

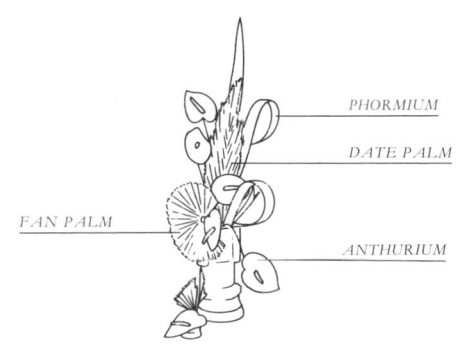

PHORMIUM

DATE PALM

FAN PALM

ANTHURIUM

POT-ET-FLEUR
(as a Mothering Sunday gift)

CREATED FOR this corner, by an upstairs window, the green and white *pot-et-fleur* looks fresh and cool. The various plants are used as an effective background for a few flowers. They looked attractive as a group before the flowers were added, an important factor in making up a successful arrangement of this kind.

The palms and ferns were favourite house plants when the portrait photograph was taken and they remain favourites today. Used as they are here, they become part of a long-lived arrangement, fresh flowers, perhaps of quite different colours and shapes, taking the place of the lilies as they fade.

SIZE
109 cm × 65 cm (41¼ in × 25½ in).

CONTAINERS
A washbowl with a willow-pattern design, 32 cm in diameter (12½ in). A round tin, 10 cm in diameter × 5 cm deep (4 in × 2 in). A well-soaked block of foam, standing 9 cm (3½ in) above the rim of the tin and taped securely to it.

EQUIPMENT
Charcoal pieces. Potting soil (compost) for indoor plants.

FOLIAGE PLANTS
Howea belmoreana (Kentia belmoreana) (sentry palm).
Howea forsteriana (Kentia forsteriana) (Kentia palm).
Dieffenbachia picta superba (dumb cane, leopard lily).
Caladium × hortulanum candidum (angel's wings).
Asplenium nidus (bird's-nest fern).
Adiantum raddianum (A. cuneatum) (delta maidenhair fern).

FLOWERS
Zantedeschia aethiopica (arum or calla lily).

ARRANGER
Jean Deas

1 Give the plants a good drink and stand to drain while the bowl is prepared. Put a good layer of charcoal pieces in the bottom of the bowl; these will keep the soil sweet for a reasonably long period. Add potting soil to cover the charcoal to a depth of about 2 cm (¾ in) and then place the tin at the front of the bowl, the top just below the rim and the foam above it, using the soil to get it level. The plants, as they are added, will hold it in position. Re-pot the dieffenbachia and the adiantum into black, plastic-bag-type polythene pots and take the other plants out of their pots but do not let them dry out.

2 Plant the two palms near the back of the bowl, the taller, sentry palm behind the Kentia palm. On the left, place the dieffenbachia well up in the bowl, packing plenty of soil underneath it so that its top leaf comes about halfway up the taller palm. Plant the caladium just in front, with its pale, strikingly veined leaves coming over the front and the side of the bowl. On the opposite side, plant the asplenium. Just behind the block of foam and raised up with soil, place the feathery-leaved adiantum. Level the soil to about 2 cm (¾ in) below the rim of the bowl but be careful not to get any in the tin. Fill this tin with water and, when the foam has stopped re-absorbing water, hide it with sprays of the adiantum leaves.

3 Add the arum lilies. Cut each stem on a slant and then all seven will go into the foam without difficulty. Start with the most tightly furled lily and use this at the top, by the sentry palm. Add three more on the right, these about half open, one coming out from the foam just above the rim of the bowl, the other two evenly spaced between this lily and the bud at the top. Take a more open lily next and add it on the left with caladium leaves as its background, then two fully open lilies, placing one in front of the highest of the dieffenbachia leaves and the other just above the adiantum plant.

DIEFFENBACHIA

KENTIA PALM

SENTRY PALM

ARUM LILY

ASPLENIUM

ADIANTUM

CALADIUM

4 Finally, check the water level in the tin, the dampness of the soil in the bowl and also in the two polythene containers. Soil should be damp to the touch but not soggy. The amount of water each plant will need while they are grouped together in this way will vary. The adiantum, especially, needs moist growing conditions but, placed where there is adequate light, out of draughts and where the atmosphere is not too dry, the group should give pleasure for several months at least—with care, very much longer.

HELLEBORES

CLEVER USE of just four kinds of preserved plant material has produced a fascinating picture. The design is attractive, the colours are subtle and everything is in perfect condition. The picture reminds us that each season has its own treasures and the clear-cut, spacious design is appropriate for flowers which bloom in the months when trees are bare and growth is slow.

SIZE
37 cm × 25½ cm (14½ in × 10 in), framed, the frame not shown, 38 cm × 48 cm (15 in × 19 in).

BACKGROUND
Pale grey-green, matt-finish fabric, pulled evenly over an oblong of hardboard and taped in place. The board is cut to fit as a back for a box-type frame.

EQUIPMENT
Glue (latex-type), tweezers and a magnifying glass.

FOLIAGE
Eucalyptus gunnii (gum tree), the juvenile leaves.
Helleborus orientalis (Lenten rose).
H. niger Christmas rose.

FLOWERS
Helleborus orientalis hybrids (Lenten rose), six.
Helleborus niger (Christmas rose), two.

OTHER PLANT MATERIAL
Cupressus glabra (Arizona cypress) cones, six.
Tendrils and two short pieces of stem from a vine.

ARRANGER
Dorothy Bye

1 Before working on the prepared background, arrange the plant material on a sheet of light-coloured paper and then, piece by piece, re-assemble the design, gluing each piece in position taking great care not to mark the background with drops or trails of glue and using the minimum to hold petal, leaf or tendril in place. Start in the centre of this design and work in a very lazy 'S' shape with the eucalyptus leaves, curving in a little to the right at the top and to the left at the bottom. None of this plant material is glued down completely and some is placed to stand out more from the background than others. Add tendrils of the vine, to the left at the top and three-quarters of the way down, also on the left, just below the top on the right and almost straight down at the bottom on the right. Add two eucalyptus leaves on the lower tendril on the left and another stem of four leaves high on the right. Complete the outline with two short pieces of vine stem placed horizontally, the lower one level with the bottom leaf on the left and directly below the top tendril's tip and the top leaf; link these two bits of stem with a curling tendril.

2 Add the cones; towards the top on the right, a cone with a smaller one on the same stem, two more completing a diagonal line between the first cone and the tendril on the left and the other two below the centre of the design and going across to the right. Now add the flowers, six, following the original 'S' curves. Start with a small pink one at the top, the next a little larger and greener. Place a rich maroon-pink flower across a little to the right and a pale pink one on its right; below this flower add a darker one. Below again place the sixth Lenten rose, a pale one and to emphasize this, add a section of a pale green leaf behind and down to the right. Finally, add two Christmas roses, one in the middle and one below, just to the right of the stems of vine. The only flower facing forward is the first of these two Christmas roses; all the others should be angled with the largest pale pink flower and the lower white one almost in profile. The picture is ready for its frame.

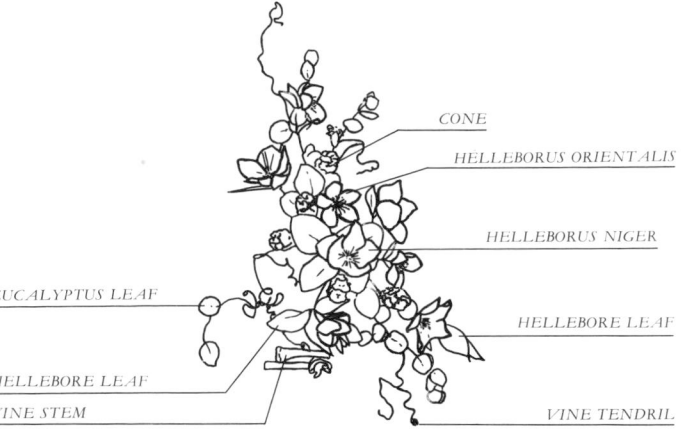

CONE

HELLEBORUS ORIENTALIS

HELLEBORUS NIGER

EUCALYPTUS LEAF

HELLEBORE LEAF

HELLEBORE LEAF

VINE STEM

VINE TENDRIL

TEDDY BEARS' PICNIC

FAVOURITE TEDDIES, invited to join the tea-party, are sitting in their own special chairs among a cascade of bright spring flowers. The whole design is light-hearted enough for adults to enjoy but serious enough, with the teddies taking pride of place, for the entertainment of the three-year-old host and his guests.

SIZE
86 cm × 56 cm (34 in × 22 in).

CONTAINERS
Two round, plastic dishes, 15 cm (6 in) and 10 cm (4 in) in diameter, both 4 cm (1½ in) deep.

EQUIPMENT
Blocks of foam, cut to fit across the dishes, standing 6 cm (2 in) above the rims.

FOLIAGE
Mahonia bealei.
Hedera helix 'Hibernica' (Irish ivy).
Chamaecyparis lawsoniana (Lawson's cypress).
Elaeagnus × ebbingei.
Euonymus japonicus mediopictus.

FLOWERS
From the florist: yellow freesias; pink spray carnations; yellow tulips.

OTHER PLANT MATERIAL
Stems of *Cornus alba* 'Siberica'.

ACCESSORIES
Three teddies. Teddy-sized deck chairs and Windsor chairs.

ARRANGER
Kevin Gunnell

1 Getting the teddies comfortably settled is most important. Angle the chairs, with the deck chair for the smallest teddy a little further forward than the Windsor chair; this will make it easy to hide the larger of the two dishes between them. This back dish is to hold the larger part of the arrangement. For the front part, put the smaller dish in line with the other and just in front of the deck chair. When it is finished, the arrangement should look as if all the plant material comes from one container.

2 Take a stem of cornus and use this bright red, twiggy material for the height at the back. Add a shorter piece just to its left and, among these stems, place a dark green mahonia leaf. To the left, add a stem of small-leafed ivy. In front of this group and from the middle teddy's shoulder downwards, add a few pieces of Lawson's cypress to make a good background for the flowers. Next, working from the second dish, bring some foliage forward over the table, cypress first

and then a stem of the smaller ivy leaves and, again to make a good background for the flowers, add a cluster of larger ivy leaves, each one placed individually.

3 Add the stem of pale elaeagnus next, putting it into the back of the arrangement, the tip just above the middle teddy's head. Then arrange the freesias in a gentle 'S' curve, starting up to the left of the cornus and continuing through the middle, curving round the smallest teddy's feet and finishing at the front of the design. Above the lowest freesias add some variegated euonymus leaves and a few more in the lower half of the back part of the arrangement. Then add the spray carnations, using them as single blooms, and the tulips, following the same curving line through both parts of the arrangement. Finally, ice the cake, light the candles—'Happy Birthday!'

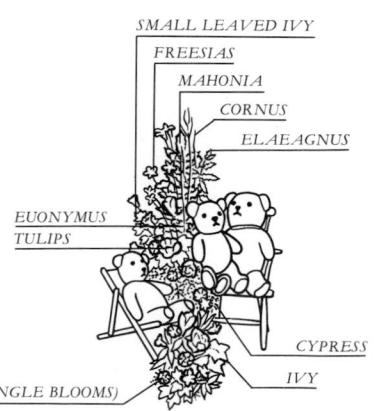

SMALL LEAVED IVY
FREESIAS
MAHONIA
CORNUS
ELAEAGNUS
EUONYMUS
TULIPS
CYPRESS
IVY
SPRAY CARNATIONS (SINGLE BLOOMS)

ENTERTAINING AT home on St. Valentine's Day seemed an excellent opportunity to use this romantic dancing figure with a few spring blooms brought home from the florist's shop. These are mixed with early flowers and interesting leaves, especially the appropriately named sweetheart ivy, from the garden.

The arrangement stands on a Sheraton-style card table and the wall behind is pale green. The design repeats the curves of the table and the mirror and the asymmetrical arrangement is more interesting than if the figure had been placed in the middle with as much plant material on one side as the other.

SIZE
84 cm × 58 cm (33 in × 23 in).

CONTAINERS
Three well-type pinholders, 9 cm, 5 cm and 4 cm (3½ in, 2 in and 1½ in) in diameter.

EQUIPMENT
The largest pinholder has a square of well-soaked foam added.

FOLIAGE
Hedera canariensis 'Gloire de Marengo' (Canary Island ivy).
Hedera helix 'Deltoides' (sweetheart ivy).
Bergenia purpurascens (Megasea).
Skimmia japonica 'Foremanii'.
Skimmia japonica 'Rubella'.
Skimmia reevesiana (S. fortunei).
Ligustrum ovalifolium 'Aureum' (golden privet).

FLOWERS
From the florist: blue iris, pink tulips and cream 'Fantasy' freesia.
From the garden: *Forsythia × intermedia* 'Spectabilis', the buds breaking into colour after forcing indoors for a week or so.
Helleborus orientalis (Lenten rose).

ACCESSORIES
A bronze figure, standing on its own plinth, 56 cm (22 in) high. Two round bases, the larger 38 cm (15 in) in diameter and covered in willow-green nylon velvet, the smaller 25 cm (10 in) and covered in pale gold nylon velvet.

ARRANGER
Betty Treweeke

ST. VALENTINE'S DAY DINNER

1 Place the smaller base off centre and to the left on top of the larger one and then position the figure on its plinth in the centre of the smaller base. Then arrange three pinholders so that the plant material will curve round the figure. Raise the middle-sized holder on a block of wood or upturned box, or similar firm but easily camouflaged stand, so that it is hidden behind and just below the top of the plinth. Put the smallest holder on the right, in front of the plinth and the largest, still on the top base, on the left but forward from the plinth.

left and, again from the top holder, a stem of the sweetheart ivy to show clearly against the wall, between the hand and the knee of the figure. This completes the outline of the design. Place a large bergenia leaf in the holder on the left to mask the plinth from view (it will also provide a good background for flowers).

2 Take a stem of forsythia and place it in the top holder to come just above the figure's head and a taller piece up at the side of the mirror. Use the ivies next, a variegated piece to curve round between the two stems of forsythia, stems of both variegated and plain out over the edges of the bases on both the right and the

3 Add the freesias, the tallest just behind the figure's head and from there curve them down and round until the last one is placed just below her foot. Group three hellebores and one more freesia on the left; this will add visual balance. Ivy and sprays of skimmia leaves with their clusters of pink and cream buds are added next on the right and among the hellebores. Add three pieces of bright gold and green privet to repeat the curve of the freesias.

4 The iris come next. Follow this same line but take one to the back of the arrangement on the left. Finally, add the five pink tulips to curve in a wider sweep round the figure, making sure her dancing movement remains an important part of the design.

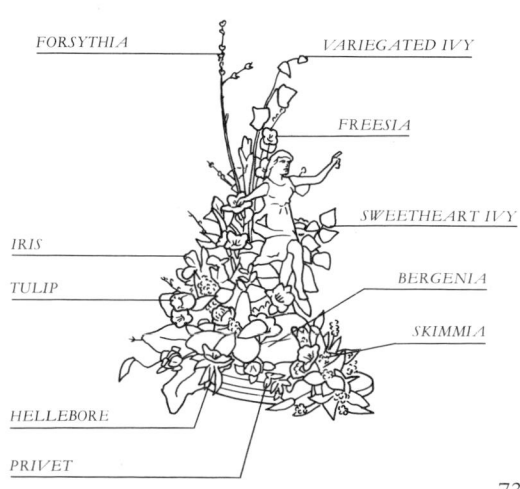

FORSYTHIA

VARIEGATED IVY

FREESIA

IRIS

SWEETHEART IVY

TULIP

BERGENIA

SKIMMIA

HELLEBORE

PRIVET

THIS DESIGN for a dinner
party has an Edwardian theme
and the imaginary guest of honour is
Lily Langtry. The two-tier arrangement suggests the abundance picked
from 19th century gardens.

SIZE
110 cm × 89 cm × 61 cm
(43½ in × 35 in × 23½ in).

CONTAINERS
A large dish, painted dull gold,
35 cm × 5 cm (13½ in × 2 in), standing on an
oval, greenish-brown silk covered base,
54 cm × 36 cm (21½ in × 14½ in). An ormulu
candlestick with a dull gold painted bowl
fixed to the top.

EQUIPMENT
A tin, 10 cm × 12 cm (4 in × 4¾ in) painted
dull gold, upturned in the dish and
surrounded by blocks of soaked foam
standing 5 cm (2 in) above the rim of the dish
and taped firmly to it. A square of foam in
the bowl on the candlestick.

FOLIAGE
Fatsia japonica (Aralia sieboldii, A.
japonica) (false castor-oil plant).
Hedera canariensis 'Gloire de Marengo'
(Canary Island ivy).
Hedera helix (English ivy).
Hedera colchica 'Sulphur Heart'
(Paddy's Pride') (Persian ivy).
Arum italicum 'Pictum'.
Iris foliage. Grasses.

FRUIT
Avocado, grapes, plums, pineapple, lime,
kumquats, apple, pear, pepper and nuts.

FLOWERS
Begonia lucerna.
Lilium longiflorum (Easter or white
trumpet lily).
Gypsophila paniculata 'Bristol fairy'
(baby's breath, chalk plant).
Anthurium scherzerianum (flamingo
flower).
Syringa vulgaris (lilac), white.
Gerbera jamesonii (Transvaal daisy,
Barberton daisy), white.
Carnations.
Chrysanthemums.

ACCESSORIES
Two plaster mouldings, sprayed dull gold.

ARRANGER
Lilian Martin

FOR LILY LANGTRY

1 Stand the candlestick
on the upturned tin,
the tin in the middle of the
dish. Place the mouldings
to rest on either side of the
dish and over the base
onto the table. Establish
the height with a stem of
grass, work round with
more, a little wider and
lower. Repeat this same
pattern with the dainty
flowers of the begonia
falling well below the
bowl.

2 In the lower section
place a fatsia leaf by
each piece of moulding,
then start placing the fruit.
This is held in place with
cocktail sticks pushed into
the foam. One stick will
hold small fruit, others
may need more. Work up
and across and then in the
opposite direction.

3 Return to the top
section. Use stems of
cream-edged ivy over the
edge of the bowl. Take
three of these 'Gloire de
Marengo' leaves, pure
cream if possible, and turn
them into the shape of an
arum lily spathe, holding

them in place with thin
wire and then wired to
cocktail sticks. Place them
round the arrangement.
Add two iris leaves, to
right and left and a lily bud
in the centre with another
ivy leaf 'lily' a little lower
on the right. Add sprays of
dainty gypsophila all
round. Follow with three
anthuriums, use these quite
high up but with short
stems, varying the levels.
Add deeper coloured
carnations and chrysanthemums to fill in any gaps. In
the lower section add some
foliage between the fruit,
both ivies, arum leaves
and, tucked in near the
table, fatsia leaves. In the
middle of the arrangement

use more of both ivies before adding flowers. Take the lilac first and place these graceful heads to fall across some of the fruit. Above them and round the arrangement use single stems of lilies and three white gerberas, one on the right near the candlestick, the other two down on the opposite side.

4 Finish the top by adding three clear yellow carnations near the anthuriums and then single stems from the lemon-coloured spray carnations.

Both kinds of carnation stay within the outline formed originally by the grasses. In the lower part of the design, emphasise the colour links with more carnations, lemon-yellow over the mouldings and the orange tipped yellow ones nearer the centre. To link the pink flowers above with this lower part add pink carnations down near the fruit on both sides and chrysanthemums higher and near the middle. Finally, with a few grasses lighten the outline.

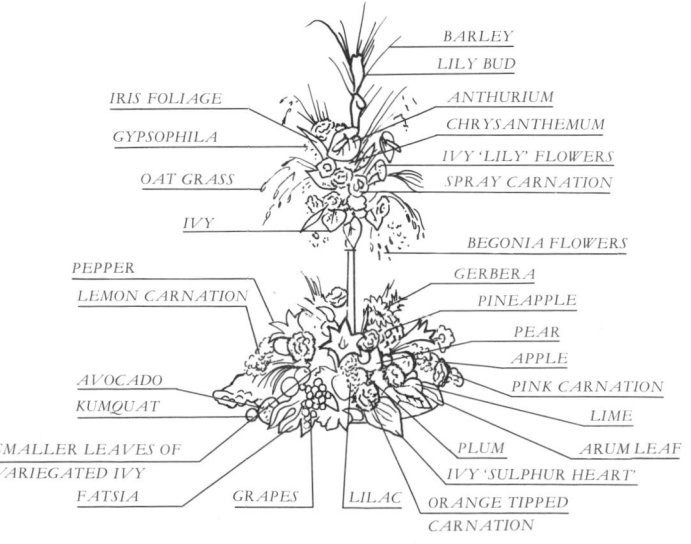

BARLEY
LILY BUD
IRIS FOLIAGE
ANTHURIUM
CHRYSANTHEMUM
GYPSOPHILA
IVY 'LILY' FLOWERS
SPRAY CARNATION
OAT GRASS
IVY
BEGONIA FLOWERS
PEPPER
GERBERA
LEMON CARNATION
PINEAPPLE
PEAR
APPLE
PINK CARNATION
LIME
AVOCADO
KUMQUAT
SMALLER LEAVES OF
VARIEGATED IVY
PLUM
ARUM LEAF
IVY 'SULPHUR HEART'
FATSIA
GRAPES
LILAC
ORANGE TIPPED
CARNATION

A SIMPLE lunch party for a few friends, on a lovely late-spring day, is the perfect excuse to use this room which looks out over the river and the fields. Three baskets, generously filled, are reflected in the shining surface of the table. Cool green and white leaves and flowers and the brightness of the lemons become part of the scene outside, fresh and summery with a light breeze over the river suggesting warmer days to follow.

SIZE
140 cm × 40½ cm (55 in × 16 in).

CONTAINERS
Three baskets with handles, 25 cm × 18 cm (10 in × 7 in), each with a plastic dish inside. One basket, without a handle, is reversed and used to raise the centre basket, 28 cm × 5 cm (11 in × 2 in).

EQUIPMENT
Blocks of soaked foam in each dish, standing above the rims by 5 cm (2 in), taped across.

FOLIAGE
Hedera colchica 'Sulphur Heart' ('Paddy's Pride') (Canary Island ivy).
Hedera helix, a variegated form (English ivy).
Hosta undulata (H. lancifolia undulata) (plantain lily).
Hosta fortunei 'Albopicta' ('Picta') (plantain lily).
Lamiastrum galeobdolon (Lamium galeobdolon, Galeobdolon luteum) (yellow archangel, golden deadnettle).
Astrantia major 'Variegata' (Masterwort).

FLOWERS
Tellima grandiflora T. odorata (fringecup).
Polygonatum × hybridum (P. multiflorum) (Solomon's seal).
Ranunculus asiaticus 'Belle Desire' (Persian or turban buttercup).
Euphorbia cyparissias (spurge).

FRUIT
Grapes, apples and lemons.

ARRANGER
Edna Johnson

1 Place the baskets on the table, equally spaced, about 25 cm (10 in) between. Work on all three together, starting with the sprays of tellima. Use these to give graduated height from the tallest point on the right-hand side of the centre basket and then finishing with stems out towards the ends of the table, establishing the length of the design. Use both kinds of ivy and both hostas to form a background for the fruit and the flowers. Bring some leaves forward and out over the edges of the baskets.

2 Take the golden dead-nettle next and add stems to the outline material. Use a stem of the Solomon's seal in the middle basket, shorter than the top stems of tellima but balancing this first placement. Two more short pieces should be added low down in the other two baskets, following the line along the table. Add an astrantia leaf on either side in the middle. As the three sections are built up make sure they do not merge together completely but form a long, low, triangular design with space between the baskets.

3 Add the fruit, each piece mounted on cocktail sticks; the grapes can be supported by putting bunches around one or more sticks placed in the foam. Use two small bunches of grapes first, one on each side of the middle basket and both

slightly off centre. Add
two lemons and two apples
to each basket and vary the
positions from one to the
other. The final material to
add is the euphorbia. With
these dainty, greenish-
yellow flowers put another
bright note here and there
in all three sections.

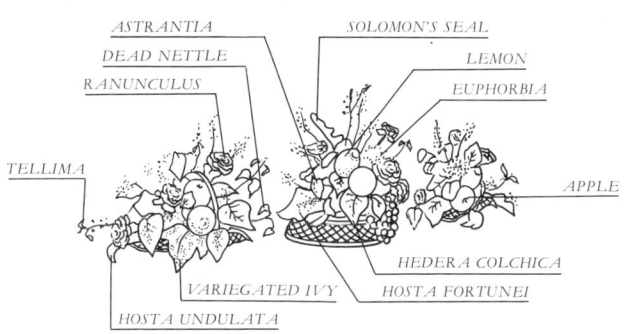

ASTRANTIA

DEAD NETTLE

RANUNCULUS

TELLIMA

SOLOMON'S SEAL

LEMON

EUPHORBIA

APPLE

HEDERA COLCHICA

VARIEGATED IVY

HOSTA FORTUNEI

HOSTA UNDULATA

TEA ON THE LAWN

A SIMPLE arrangement of garden flowers which adds its charm to the peaceful scene. The delicacy of the pastel colours and varied forms all blend together delightfully, adding to the occasion and the setting.

SIZE
35½ cm × 29 cm (14 in × 11½ in). The table is 91 cm (36 in) in diameter.

CONTAINER
A silver sugar-bowl stand, 13 cm × 9 cm (5 in × 3½ in) with a plastic dish fitted inside.

EQUIPMENT
A block of foam, standing 4 cm (1½ in) above the rim of the dish and taped to it.

FOLIAGE
None except that on the stems of flowers.

FLOWERS
Weigela variegata (Diervilla).
Oxypetalum caeruleum (Tweedia caerutea) (southern star).
Apple blossom.
Aquilegia vulgaris (wild columbine, granny's bonnet).
Aquilegia × hybrida (columbine).
Clematis montana rubens.
Convallaria majalis (lily of the valley).
Dicentra spectabilis (Bleeding heart).
Dianthus × allwoodii 'Doris' (pinks).

ARRANGER
Sylvia Lewis

1 With stems of weigela, form an easy flowing outline. Remove any surplus leaves which will make the arrangement look heavy when it is complete but choose two stems to come down over the edge of the container which have good curves and perfect foliage. Use one at the front on the right and the other at the back, in a similar position. Add some of the clear blue tweedia flowers, using their graceful stems to follow the outline, remembering the arrangement will be seen from all round. Add clusters of apple blossom low down at the front and the back and another, taller stem, in the middle.

2 Use both kinds of columbine next, the larger pale flowers through the middle from the very top, the smaller, granny's bonnets, towards the outside on the left and then coming right into the middle. Low down in the arrangement use the darkest of these small flowers. The darker pink flowers on the left balance the leafy piece of weigela on the right.

3 Take two short stems of clematis and place one at the front and one at the back, both to come over the rim of the container with weigela leaves behind. Add stems of lily of the valley in and out of the design, some nearly as tall as the outline stems and some tucked in between flower heads. Two sprays of dicentra repeat the darker pink. Fill in the design with a few pinks, using buds to the outside and fully opened flowers on quite short stems nearer the middle, just a few, well spaced out through the arrangement, so that the dainty effect is not lost.

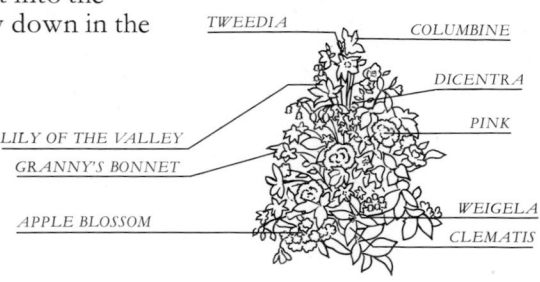

TWEEDIA — COLUMBINE
DICENTRA
PINK
LILY OF THE VALLEY
GRANNY'S BONNET
WEIGELA
APPLE BLOSSOM — CLEMATIS

TWENTY-FIFTH ANNIVERSARY

AN ARRANGEMENT for a special luncheon party to celebrate a twenty-fifth wedding anniversary. The table is circular and so the design chosen gives equal pleasure from all round.

The soft textures and colours of the flowers and foliage in white, pink and grey have a touch of shining pinkish-brown added to repeat the colour of the vine leaves.

SIZE
48 cm × 37 cm (19 in × 15 in).

CONTAINER
White porcelain Copeland lamp base with cherubs supporting the bowl, 14 cm × 14 cm (5½ in × 5½ in). A soft green, velvet covered base, cut to the exact shape of the foot of the container, is added. This is edged with braid and is about 2 cm (¾ in) deep.

EQUIPMENT
A third of a block of foam is fixed with tape to a small bowl. This is fitted securely inside the top of the container.

FOLIAGE
Eucalyptus gunnii (gum tree).
Convolvulus cneorum.
Senecio bicolor (S. cineraria, S. maritimus, Cineraria bicolor, C. maritima) (silver-leaved cineraria or dusty miller).
Dorycnium hirsutum (Canary clover) with its seed-heads.
Echeveria.
Vitis vinifera 'Brandt' (grape vine).

FLOWERS
Cluster rose (Floribunda) 'Isis'.
Florists' rose 'Pitika'.
Florists' spray carnations in pale pink.

OTHER PLANT MATERIAL
Grapes and peaches.

ARRANGER
José Allen

1 Place five sprays of eucalyptus round the rim of the container, giving a soft all round design and avoiding any too obvious repetition of the shape of the foot of the container. Then add five stems of the convolvulus between the eucalyptus and for the tallest point.

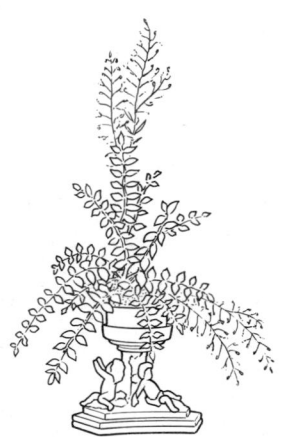

2 Rosettes of echeveria and senecio leaves can then be positioned towards the centre, following the all round design again.

Stems of the dorycnium, with their shining pinkish-brown seed-heads, are tucked in to add interest.

3 Then come the roses, both 'Isis' and 'Pitika', and the spray carnations. A few of the rose leaves are removed to keep the colour emphasis on white, pink and grey. These flowers have a bolder form than the foliage. They add a soft but noticeable contrast of colour and they are in scale with the rest of the arrangement, linking it to the shape and style of the container.

A bunch of green grapes will conceal a tiny water-filled tube into which the stem of the vine can be placed. The cut peach is photographer's licence but its colours blend beautifully with the curtains, the colours in the cloth and the tint of the same colour in the 'Pitika' roses. Add another bunch of grapes and a few vine leaves on the opposite side of the arrangement and the table is ready to be set for the party.

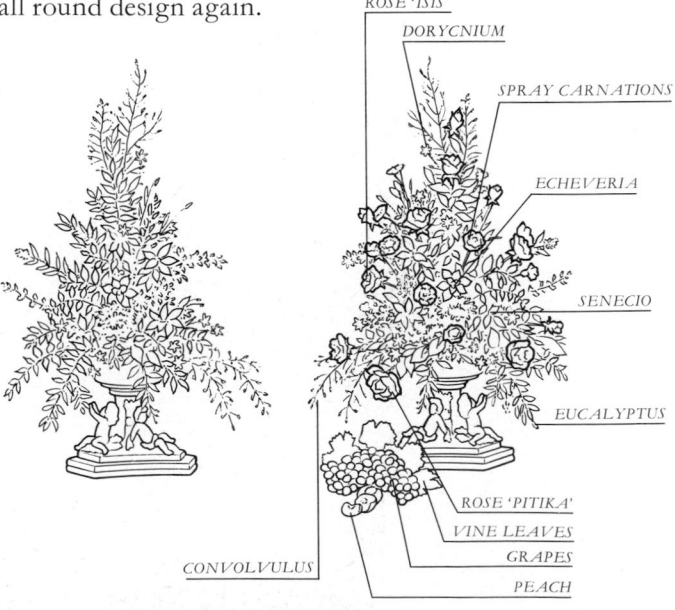

ROSE 'ISIS'
DORYCNIUM
SPRAY CARNATIONS
ECHEVERIA
SENECIO
EUCALYPTUS
ROSE 'PITIKA'
VINE LEAVES
GRAPES
PEACH
CONVOLVULUS

THE CHRISTMAS TABLE

BEAUTIFUL FRESH carnations, some with delicately fringed edges to their petals, are a striking feature of this arrangement on a long rosewood table. Baubles and glittered leaves suggest the sparkle of Christmas and add to the enjoyment of light reflected in the simple but elegant shapes of the glasses and candlesticks. More baubles and bells exactly match the little parcels.

The blue of the china and the table linen is picked up again by the candles and this soft blue, with the pink, cerise and silver of the arrangement, is part of an unusual colour scheme for a centuries-old celebration in a modern home.

SIZE
140 cm × 41 cm (55 in × 16 in).

CONTAINER
Plastic dish designed to hold foam, 15 cm (6 in) in diameter.

EQUIPMENT
Oblong of foam, cut to fit across the dish and placed lengthways on the table.

FOLIAGE
Mahonia bealei leaves, glycerined and then sprayed a dull silver.
Cotoneaster franchetii.
Chamaecyparis lawsoniana (Lawson's cypress), some sprayed with artificial snow and some lightly painted white.

FLOWERS
Pink spray carnations and pink, large-bloomed, fimbriated carnations.

ARTIFICIAL PLANT MATERIAL
Sprays of white leaves, silver glittered.
Baubles and bells.

ACCESSORIES
Small parcels, wrapped and decorated to match.
Optional extra: oval base covered in pale blue material, 69 cm × 30 cm (27 in × 12 in).

ARRANGER
Mavis Brooker

1 If the base is to be used, position this first, with the container on top, making sure that both are central on the table. The design is kept long and relatively narrow, using two sprays of the artificial leaves to give the length of the arrangement. Mahonia and cotoneaster stems are added next, placed so that they come down towards the table in easy, flowing lines. Use the reverse side of the cotoneaster, showing the undersides of the leaves which are a lovely, silvery grey. In the middle a few short pieces of whitened cypress will mask the foam.

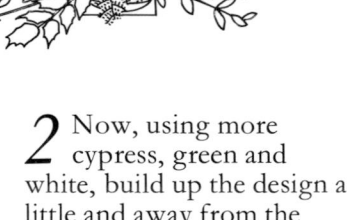

2 Now, using more cypress, green and white, build up the design a little and away from the table, creating a background for the flowers. Put the first bauble near the centre, quite low down. Recessed like this, it still reflects some light and carries the silver colour through the design.

3 Next, start placing in position the smaller spray blooms of the carnations, following the lines established by the foliage. The larger flowers

follow and then a few more of the small ones are tucked in towards the centre, blending the two sizes together within the design.

4 Finally, the deep cerise and silver baubles and the bells are tucked in among the paler carnations, still following the lines of the first pieces of foliage. A few more are placed along the table.

ARTIFICIAL LEAVES LARGER CARNATION SPRAY CARNATIONS

MAHONIA BAUBLE BELL
COTONEASTER CYPRESS

Boxing Day

A SILVER punch bowl stands on a lovingly polished 17th century oak table ready to welcome guests to a Boxing Day party. Four decorated stands add to the festive setting.

Deeper shades of the colours in the curtains are used—apricot, orange and green. White flowers suggest snow-flakes and there are tiny red, gold and silver baubles.

SIZE
84 cm × 40 cm (33 in × 16 in); 56 cm × 28 cm (22 in × 11 in).

CONTAINERS
Four stands, finished in matt black, made of iron rods, are fixed to round metal bowls. These are bought ready-made. The larger pair of stands is 61 cm (24 in) high; the smaller pair is 41 cm (16 in) high. The bowls, three on each stand, graduate in size with the largest at each stand base being 20 cm (8 in) and 14 cm (5½ in) in diameter respectively.

EQUIPMENT
Pieces of foam cut to fit firmly in each bowl, as much showing above the rim as below.

FOLIAGE
Chamaecyparis lawsoniana (Lawson's cypress) in green and blue-green forms.
Ilex aquifolium 'Silver Queen', and 'Golden Queen' (hollies).
Erica arborea alpina (tree heath).
Hedera helix 'Glacier' (ivy).
Eucalyptus mitchelliana (gum tree, weeping sally).

FLOWERS
Spray carnations in three shades of soft orange.
Single spray white chrysanthemums.

ACCESSORIES
Christmas baubles, tiny parcels, stars and silver bells, all mounted on stub wires and this covered with tape.

ARRANGER
Pamela McNichol

1 First establish the height and width of all four arrangements, the shorter pair being approximately two-thirds the height and width of the larger pair. Use eucalyptus to give the height and lightness to the outline with its slender stems and long narrow leaves. The cypress foliage can then be used for contrast and it will help to cover the foam. Small pieces of holly, ivy and the tree heath are tucked in, adding more variety of texture and colour. Grade the width of each tier carefully so that the stands turn into airy, triangular tree shapes.

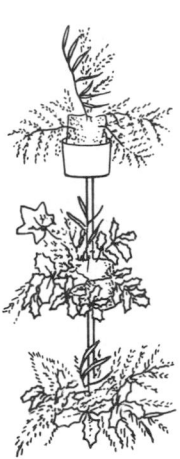

2 Use the carnations next and then the white chrysanthemums, mostly as single stems, again following the established outline, making sure each bowl has about the same amount of colour as the others.

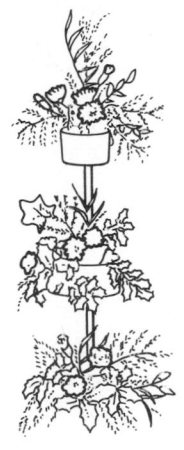

3 Add the baubles last, the red giving depth of colour and the silver and gold some sparkle. Finally the punch bowl is filled and placed on a silver tray.

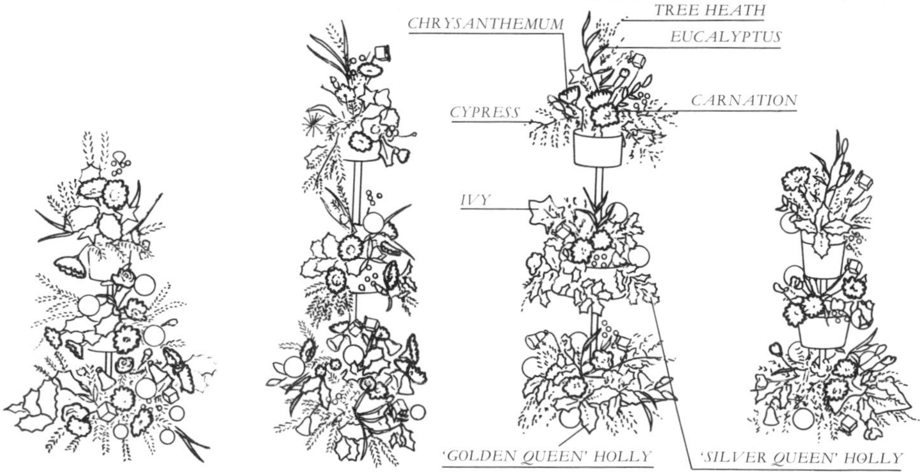

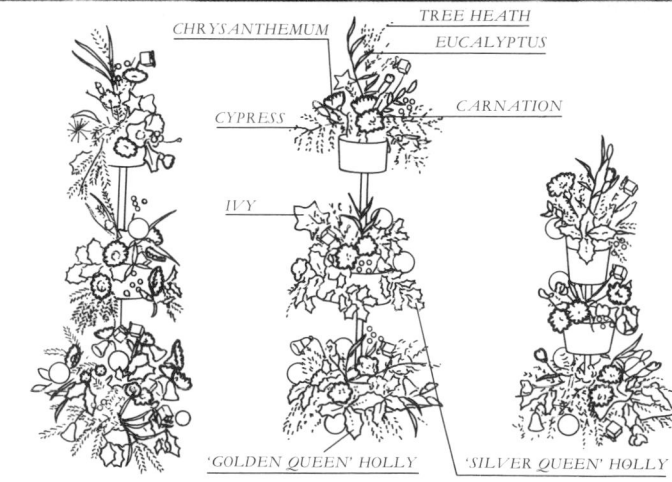

CHRYSANTHEMUM   TREE HEATH

EUCALYPTUS

CYPRESS   CARNATION

IVY

'GOLDEN QUEEN' HOLLY   'SILVER QUEEN' HOLLY

FOR THE BRIDE

REFLECTED IN the mirror, this little arrangement is designed for the bride as she prepares for the marriage ceremony and, later, when she changes before leaving for the honeymoon. It picks up colours chosen for the wedding, especially the soft cream of the lace veil and the pink and blue of the posies carried by the bridesmaids and the decorations on the pew ends. The next two arrangements (for a church window and pew end) were designed for the same wedding colour scheme.

SIZE
48 cm × 40½ cm (19 in × 16 in).

CONTAINER
A silver basket, 15 cm × 11½ cm × 17½ cm to the top of the handle (6½ in × 4½ in × 7 in). The basket stands on a footed, silver tray with a pie-crust edge, 14½ cm (5¾ in) across. A round base covered in ecru-coloured velvet and edged with dull pink braid, 21 cm (8½ in) in diameter.

EQUIPMENT
The silver basket is lined with foil before adding a block of foam, which stands 4 cm (1½ in) above the rim of the basket.

FOLIAGE
Trifolium repens (clover, variegated form).
Ruta graveolens 'Variegata' (rue).

FLOWERS
Heucherella 'Bridget Bloom' (Heuchera × Tiarella).
Nigella damascena (love-in-a-mist).
Rose 'Cecile Brunner'.

ARRANGER
Norah Phillippo

1 Place the base, slightly raised on an upturned tin, centrally in front of the mirror and add the tray and the basket. Form the triangular outline with the heucherella and then use the variegated clover leaves, following the same lines but on quite short stems.

2 Follow these lines again with the rue, choosing stems with as little green as possible, then add the nigella, placing these slightly shorter stems in the triangular pattern. The thread-like bracts on their stems among the rue and the clover should be sufficient to mask the foam but, if not, cut some short pieces of the rue and tuck these in low down.

3 Add the roses through the middle of the arrangement and to both sides with some attractively reflected in the mirror. Finally, make sure the foam does not show in the mirror. Cover it with a little more foliage or a rosebud if it does.

86

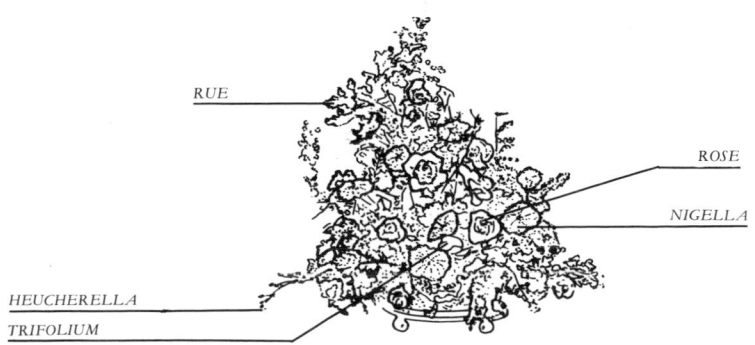

RUE

ROSE

NIGELLA

HEUCHERELLA

TRIFOLIUM

A CHURCH WINDOW

THE BLUE and green of the stained glass in the window and the cream colour of the stone are repeated in the arrangement. The pure white lilies add their elegance, and the pale cream peonies have a quite different shape, their colour linking the white to the dark cream aruncus.

SIZE
178 cm × 147½ cm × 66 cm
(70 in × 58 in × 26 in).

CONTAINER
A large black tin,
30½ cm × 30½ cm × 12½ cm
(12 in × 12 in × 5 in), designed and made for this type of arrangement.

EQUIPMENT
Two bricks, to stabilize the weight of the arrangement, placed at the back of the container. Six blocks of foam, used upright. Wire netting, 5 cm (2 in) mesh, taken over the top of the container and foam and fixed on all four sides at the holes provided. A metal cone, taped to a cane, with a small piece of crumpled wire netting inside and hooked over the rim securely.

FOLIAGE
Polystichum setiferum (soft shield or hedge fern).
Hosta plantaginea (plantain lily).
Polygonatum commutatum (P. giganteum) (giant Solomon's seal).
Cotinus coggygria 'Royal Purple'.
Berberis thunbergii 'Atropurpurea' (Japanese barberry).

FLOWERS
Delphiniums.
Philadelphus coronarius (mock orange).
Aruncus dioicus (A. sylvester, A. vulgaris) (goat's beard).
Lilium longiflorum (white trumpet lily, Easter lily).
Alchemilla mollis (lady's mantle).
Paeonia lactiflora 'Bowl of Cream' (peony).

ARRANGER
Evelyn Mercer

1 Place the container to the left of the window sill, bricks at the back and foam at the front. With a tall, pale blue delphinium establish the height of the finished arrangement. To do this use a metal cone, placing it in the foam towards the back with the flower just to the left of the glass. Form an undulating fan shape with the ferns, against the stone on the left, across the window and down on the right to the edge of the sill. On either side, low in the arrangement add branching stems of phila-delphus foliage and then a few stems of the flowers (leaves removed to extend their life). At the back, to the left of the delphinium, add a tall, straight stem of philadelphus foliage, to the right a stem of aruncus. Two short stems of delphiniums will complete the basic shape of the arrangement. Place one on the left, between two ferns, the other on the right, above the lowest fern.

2 Before adding more delphiniums and aruncus use the large hosta leaves in the heart of the arrangement for contrast of colour and form. Group these from the centre-left through to the right, with two going back towards the window on the right to give depth to the design. Add the delphiniums, some near the window, others in the centre and placed to come forward from the background material. Do not lose the shape of the outline. Then, place a stem of Solomon's seal so that it overhangs the window-sill and another low down on the left.

3 Add purple-leaved foliage—the cotinus and berberis—a tall stem of cotinus in front of the first delphinium and a shorter one towards the back on the left. Place shorter stems of berberis in the middle and slightly larger ones out to the right, in front of and round the hostas. Add the lilies, making full use of their long, graceful stems with the flowers coming forward from the del-phiniums and the foliage. Place one in front of the tallest delphinium; it may help if it is put in the tube with the first flower. Put another stem below it, and then one to the right to show clearly in front of the glass. With the other stems work across from the left down to the right. Finally, add some lady's mantle near the centre and the peonies, quite low in the arrangement, where they add contrast of shape and balancing visual weight.

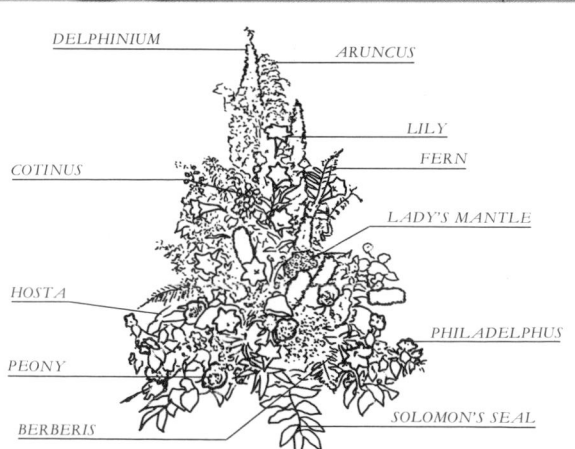

DELPHINIUM

ARUNCUS

LILY

FERN

COTINUS

LADY'S MANTLE

HOSTA

PHILADELPHUS

PEONY

BERBERIS

SOLOMON'S SEAL

89

CONTINUING THE cream, pink and blue colour scheme of this wedding, the guests are welcomed to the church with decorations on every other pew end, alternately placed to right and left, along the centre aisle. The dark foliage, used as a background, makes a good foil for the flowers with the pale oak of the pews behind.

SIZE
63½ cm × 25¼ cm × 16½ cm
(25 in × 10 in × 6½ in).

CONTAINER
A plastic, shovel-shaped holder, 15 cm × 10 cm (6 in × 4 in), excluding the handle.

EQUIPMENT
A well-soaked block of foam cut to fit the holder and standing 4 cm (1½ in) above the rim, taped in place. Leave this hanging up to drain off the surplus water before covering completely with thin polythene. This covering will protect the pew and the floor and will help to retain moisture for the stem ends—which will go through thin plastic quite easily. The handle is attached to the pew end by making a wire hook and covering this with tape or, if there is a fixing on the pew end, with thin wire.

FOLIAGE
Acer palmatum 'Atropurpurem'.
Cotinus coggygria (Rhus cotinus) 'Royal Purple' (Venetian sumach, European smoke tree/bush).

FLOWERS
Achillea taygetea (yarrow).
Aruncus dioicus (A. sylvester, A. vulgaris) (goat's beard).
Polygonum campanulatum (knotweed).
Delphiniums.
Philadelphus coronarius (mock orange).
Nicotiana 'Sensation Mixed' (flowering tobacco).
Gypsophila paniculata 'Bristol Fairy' (baby's breath, chalk plant).
Dianthus × allwoodii 'Doris' (pink).
Rose 'Pink Favourite'.

ARRANGER
Evelyn Mercer

DECORATION FOR A PEW END

1 Place stems of acer at the back of the foam at top and bottom, to lie close to the pew end. These stems establish the length and the top one hides the wire fixing the holder to the pew. In the middle, form a rosette of dark cotinus leaves and behind these, at both sides, tuck in short stems of the small cream-coloured achillea heads. Continue adding cream with sprays of aruncus, to the top and bottom and round the centre behind the cotinus. In front of these last, place the pink polygonum.

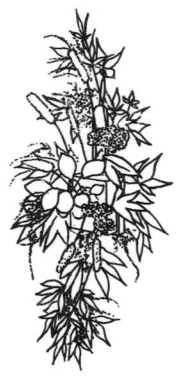

2 Use delphiniums next, two stems to accentuate the length of the design among the polygonum and aruncus and very short, lateral stems near the centre. Coming forward, in the middle of the arrangement, place

some philadelphus flowers and, at either side of these and below, a few single nicotiana flowers. Using quite short stems, add an airy sprinkling of the tiny white gypsophila.

3 Finally, add the 'Doris' pinks, covering any foam which shows, using them on short stems near the centre but longer out to the sides here and there. Then place three deep pink roses, one in the middle and two a little lower. Using these richer-coloured and larger flowers low in the arrangement will give balance to the whole design.

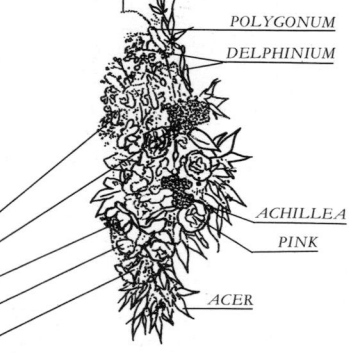

ARUNCUS
POLYGONUM
DELPHINIUM
GYPSOPHILA
COTINUS
ROSE
PHILADELPHUS
NICOTIANA
ACHILLEA
PINK
ACER

ALONGSIDE THE register and the bouquet is a little arrangement placed in the vestry for the moment when the groom, his bride and the witnesses to the marriage will sign the register.

SIZE
43 cm × 30½ cm (17 in × 12 in).

CONTAINER
A small, round alabaster bowl, 12½ cm × 15 cm (5 in × 6 in). Two round bases, covered in ecru-coloured velvet and edged with soft pink braid, 20 cm and 15 cm (8 in × 6 in) in diameter.

EQUIPMENT
A plastic dish placed inside the bowl with a square block of foam, well soaked and standing 5 cm (2 in) above the rim of the bowl.

FOLIAGE
Vinca minor 'Aureo-variegata Alba' (lesser periwinkle, trailing myrtle).
Ruta graveolens 'Variegata' (rue).
Chrysanthemum parthenium 'Aureum' *(Matricaria eximia)* (feverfew).

FLOWERS
Lonicera × tellmanniana (honeysuckle, woodbine).
Miniature roses 'Baby Masquerade', 'Pour Toi'.
Aquilegia × hybrida (long-spurred columbine).

ARRANGER
Norah Phillippo

The bouquet, designed to have a graceful and natural curve when held, uses the minimum of wire in its make-up.

FOLIAGE
Hosta fortunei 'Aurea'.
Glechoma hederacea 'Variegata' *(Nepeta glechoma, N. hederacea)* (variegated ground ivy).

FLOWERS
Aquilegia × hybrida.
Dianthus × allwoodii 'Doris'.
Miniature rose 'Pour Toi'.
Chrysanthemum 'Penny Lane'.
Aruncus dioicus (A. sylvester, A. vulgaris) (goat's beard).
Lilies, cream.

ARRANGER
Graeme Audrain

IN THE VESTRY

1 With the periwinkle and the rue make a flowing outline, the periwinkle coming out and down over the edge of the container and establishing the height and also the width of the arrangement. The rue, slightly shorter, with its pale cream leaves, plays an equally important part in forming the outline. In front of the periwinkle use the orange-yellow honeysuckle flowers on their curving stems and put one short stem, with its wide green calyx, in the centre where it will hide much of the foam.

back on both sides. Use the 'Baby Masquerade' roses next. One behind the top stem of honeysuckle, one very low down at the front, the others here and there throughout the design, remembering to take some of this colour round at the sides.

2 Add the bright yellow leaves of the feverfew to build up the middle of the design ready for the roses to be added. Add a little at the front, just to the left of the last piece of honeysuckle and other stems towards the

3 Add some clear yellow columbines, one just above the shortest stem of honeysuckle, three near the very top of the arrangement and two more, one round at each side. Lastly add the 'Pour Toi' roses, a very fully open flower near the centre front and then a slightly staggered line of five, diagonally across from left down to right, the top one turned towards the left and the bottom one turning to the right. Add another rosebud low on the left and one above it, recessed in between two brighter roses.

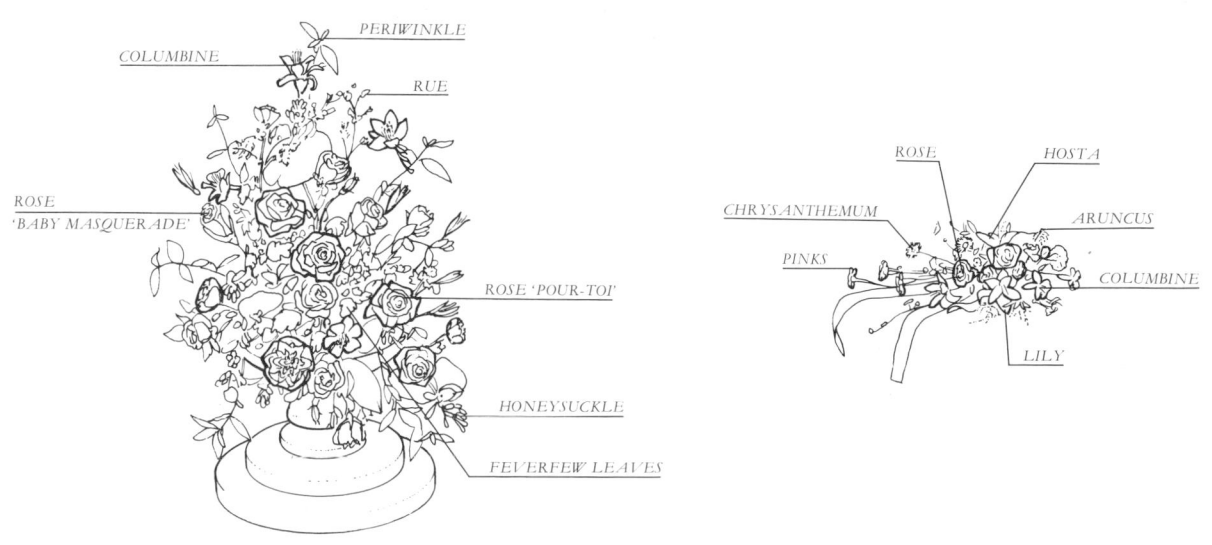

COLUMBINE

PERIWINKLE

RUE

ROSE
'BABY MASQUERADE'

ROSE 'POUR-TOI'

HONEYSUCKLE

FEVERFEW LEAVES

ROSE

HOSTA

CHRYSANTHEMUM

ARUNCUS

PINKS

COLUMBINE

LILY

THE CHURCH, which dates from 1850, is an excellent example of the architecture and craftsmanship of the period. The windows have slender, soaring lines, the carving behind the altar is finely detailed and the gold and green frontal was made for the church at the time it was built. All these features influenced the design and colours of the arrangement.

SIZE
304 cm × 178 cm × 102 cm
(120 in × 70 in × 40 in).

CONTAINER
Black wrought-iron pedestal with a flat platform top, 142 cm (56 in) high. Plant-pot saucer, 25½ cm × 6½ cm (10 in × 2½ in).

EQUIPMENT
Blocks of foam, one fitting across the saucer and half a block in front, standing 12½ cm (5 in) above the rim. 2½ cm (1 in) mesh wire netting across the foam and over the dish, wired to the top curves of iron supporting the platform. Two metal cones taped to canes which have been painted green; oblongs of well-soaked foam (standing just above the cone rims) leaving room for water to be added.

FOLIAGE
Elaeagnus pungens 'Limelight'.
Polygonatum commutatum (P. giganteum) (giant Solomon's seal).
Stephanandra incisa (S. flexuosa).
Euonymus japonicus 'Latifolius Variegatus' (Macrophyllus Albus) (Japanese spindle).
Hosta sieboldiana (H. glauca) (plantain lily).

FLOWERS
Delphiniums.
Alchemilla mollis (lady's mantle).
Cornus kousa (Benthamidia japonica, Benthamia japonica) (dogwood).
Gladioli, white.
Iris spuria hybrid, 'Sierra Nevada'.
Scabiosa caucasica (scabious, pincushion flower).
Hydrangea, white.
Matthiola incana 'Excelsior' strain (column stocks), cream.
Lilies, cream.
Carnations, golden-yellow.
Zantedeschia aethiopica (arum or calla lily).

ARRANGER
Graeme Audrain

AT THE HIGH ALTAR

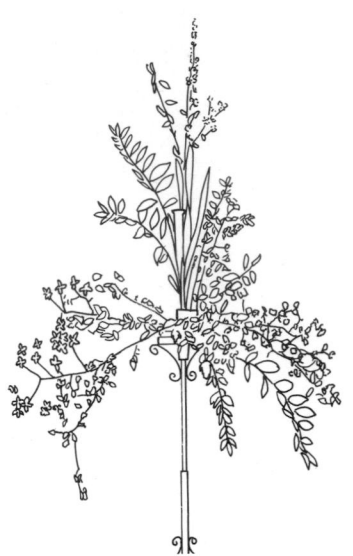

1 Place the pedestal forward and to the left of the altar, leaving room for the flowing outer stems to be placed diagonally across between the wall and the front corner of the altar. Position the two cones, one above and behind the other, slightly to the back of the centre of the container. Use gladiolus leaves between the two to hide the higher cone from the front view. In this top cone place a tall delphinium and a spray of alchemilla on its right. In the lower one place a stem of elaeagnus and two more pointed gladiolus leaves. To the sides of the cones, on the left, use two long stems of Solomon's seal, reversed to show their interesting form, then, on the right, a stem of elaeagnus, below it a stem of branching stephanandra to curve out and, below it again, a shorter stem of elaeagnus. Well out to the right, flowing down, place another stem of Solomon's seal with a fourth, nearer to the container, low at the front. This time show the front of the leaves. Behind this last leaf add a short stem of brightly variegated euonymus. On the left, take a graceful branch of the cornus (all the leaves removed to show the dainty flower-like bracts) well over towards the wall with a long spray of stephanandra leaves coming well below it.

2 Group the hosta leaves to come forward from the middle of the front piece of foam and up towards the right. Next work from the top, through the centre of the design, with delphiniums; their colour and shape will suggest a repetition of the slender window and the blue glass. Among these flowers place some iris and gladioli, using the tubes for height. Below these, on both sides, add a few scabious to carry the blue through the design. Bring stems of alchemilla right the way down on the right-hand side, a little in the middle and one spray in front of the cornus on the left.

3 Add hydrangeas and stocks on the right and cream-coloured lilies on the left but with some brought through to the right, above and between

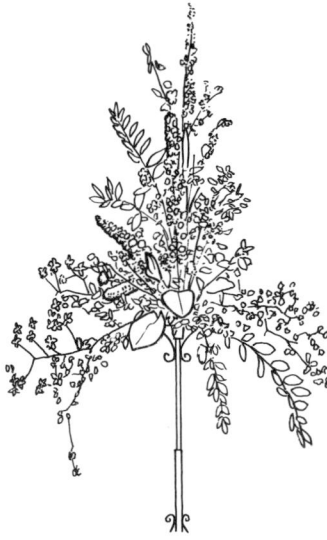

the two Solomon's seal stems. Two more lilies are placed up on the right near the irises. Next add the carnations from quite high on the left, across the centre in an easy flowing line, finishing low on the right. Complete the arrangement with the arum lilies, starting near the rich blue delphinium in the middle, coming down in front of the hosta leaves and finishing with two blooms in front of the pedestal stem.

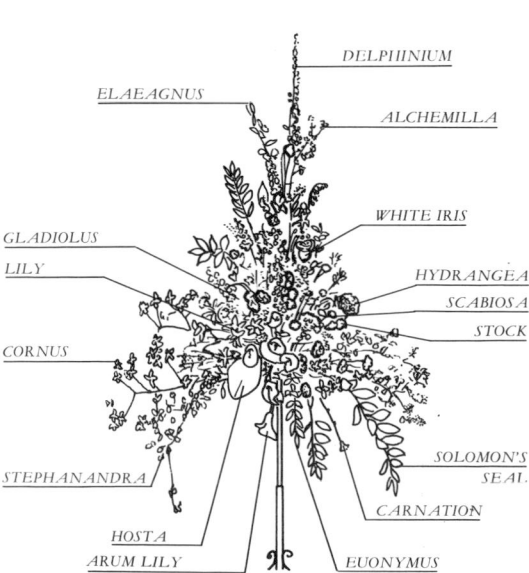

THE COLOURS of the arrangement repeat those of the pedestal by the altar but with more emphasis on green. The handsome leaves and spathes play an important part in this arrangement, which is seen from several viewpoints. They are in keeping with the bold stonework of the pulpit and, without them, there would be a tendency for the lower part of the design to be lost against the pattern and colours of the floor tiles.

The arrangement is placed on the floor and the tallest point is kept close to the pulpit. A tall, free-standing arrangement in this position would hide the pulpit with its interesting handrail.

SIZE
117 cm × 140 cm (46 in × 55 in).

CONTAINER
A large plastic bowl, 33 cm × 12½ cm (13 in × 5 in).

EQUIPMENT
Four blocks of foam, covered with 2½ cm (1 in) wire netting, firmly taped to the bowl. One metal cone securely taped to a cane; an oblong of well-soaked foam is fixed inside, leaving room for water to be added.

FOLIAGE
Fagus sylvatica 'Riversii' (Rivers' Purple) (copper beech).
Elaeagnus pungens 'Limelight'.
Elaeagnus × ebbingei.
Osmunda regalis (royal fern).
Hosta sieboldiana (H. glauca) (plantain lily).
Euonymus japonicus 'Latifolius Albomarginatus', 'Latifolius Variegatus' (Macrophyllus Albus) (Japanese spindle).

FLOWERS
Delphiniums, shades of blue.
Alchemilla mollis (lady's mantle).
Gladioli, white.
Zantedeschia 'Green Goddess', green, white-centred spathe (arum or calla lily). Lilies, cream and apricot.
Hydrangeas, white.
Iris spuria hybrid, 'Sierra Nevada'.
Scabiosa caucasica (scabious, pincushion flower), blue.
Carnations, gold and pale apricot.
Peonies, white, in bud.
Rose 'Circus'.

ARRANGER
Graeme Audrain

BY THE PULPIT

1 Place the bowl to the left of the pulpit, in the angle it makes with the steps. Use a very dark delphinium for the highest point and place this, with a stem of white gladiolus, in the cone, putting this towards the back of the foam. On both sides use branches of copper beech to curve down to the floor and a third piece behind the cone. On the left of this third piece place a long stem of *Elaeagnus* 'Limelight'. To the right, above and in front of the beech, place two fronds of the fern and behind this beech another stem of the variegated elaeagnus. Take a stem of gladiolus leaves and put this just in front of the cane to which the cone is taped; the narrow fan of leaves will hide it from view.

2 With the large hosta leaves and the handsome lily spathes give depth and interest on the left. Use this plant material in a curving line, from the left of the tube, round and down to the floor and then add a final spathe to turn in towards the central stems from the right. In the heart of this grouping of green and white, add a stem of cream lilies, another in front of the lower fern and a third between the hostas on the left. Add two hydrangea heads, one behind the lowest spathe and the other out to its right. Now work round the outside of the arrangement from the left, starting with alchemilla just above the beech. Add *Elaeagnus × ebbingei* between the two stems of alchemilla and the variegated elaeagnus. Near the top, add a further stem of alchemilla (from the cone) with a bright, golden piece of elaeagnus. In the centre add a delphinium and, lower, two more to show clearly against the stone. Placed so that it will curve round towards the base of the pulpit, use a brightly variegated and branched piece of euonymus. Complete this stage of the arrangement with another delphinium in the middle,

IN LOVING MEMORY OF
BY HIS WIDOW

a white iris on its left and right and a group of scabious low down on the left, one placed higher to carry the blue through to the delphiniums.

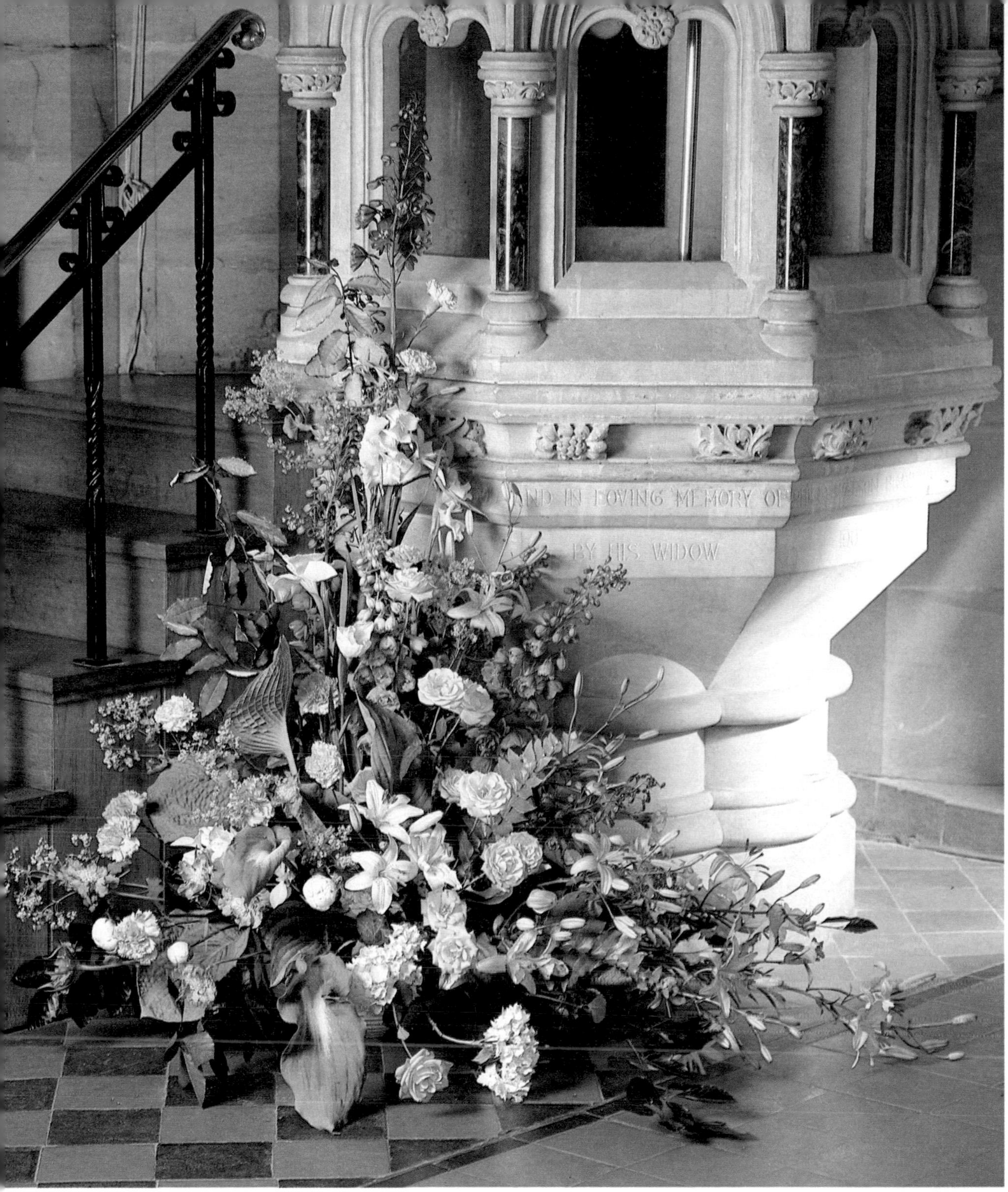

3 Add the apricot-coloured lilies out on the right. On the left, continue this colour: use both shades of carnations and add two of the golden ones near the top delphinium but on its right. Take the three peony buds from the middle towards the left and complete the design with a generous line of the golden, orange-tipped roses through from the centre, towards the right and back to the centre again between the lily spathe and the hydrangea.

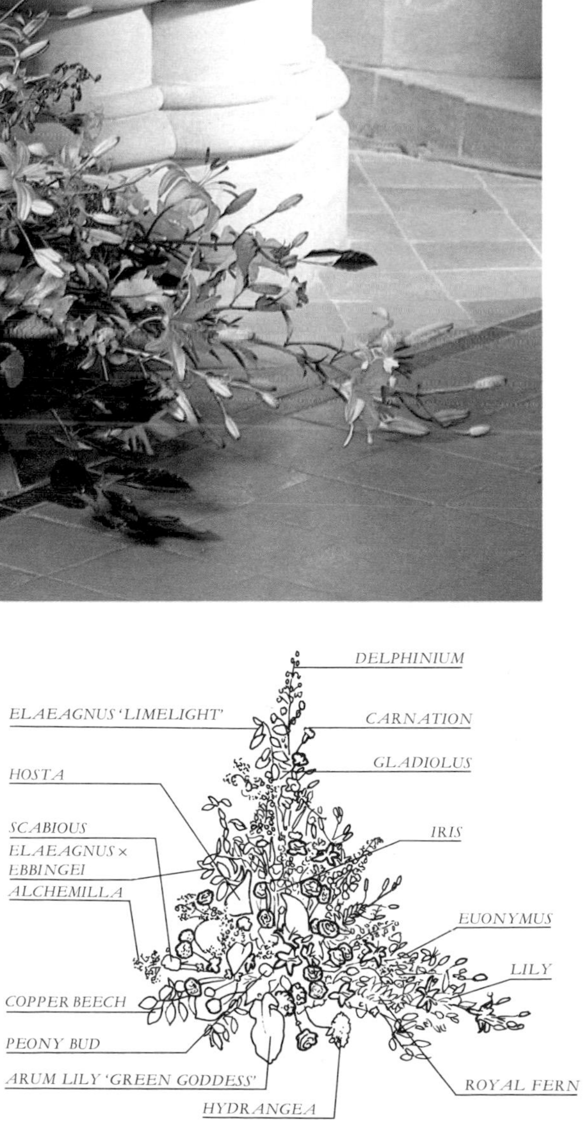

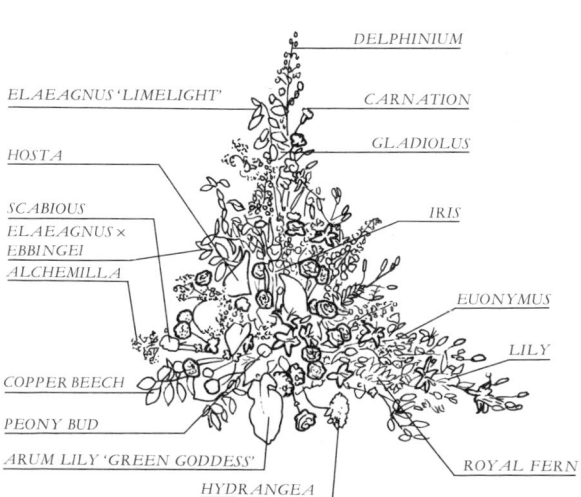

DELPHINIUM
ELAEAGNUS 'LIMELIGHT'
CARNATION
GLADIOLUS
HOSTA
SCABIOUS
IRIS
ELAEAGNUS × EBBINGEI
ALCHEMILLA
EUONYMUS
LILY
COPPER BEECH
PEONY BUD
ARUM LILY 'GREEN GODDESS'
ROYAL FERN
HYDRANGEA

THE GUESTS, waiting to be received by the wedding party, can enjoy this lovely arrangement. Its colours, the container and the rococo base, its style and scale, are all chosen to complement the room and the beautiful early 18th century English tapestries. The gold plinth standing on the dark base lifts the arrangement up from the piano and this space gives lightness to the design.

SIZE
124 cm × 114 cm × 86 cm
(49 in × 45 in × 34 in).

CONTAINER
French porcelain, white with gold decoration, 25½ cm × 20½ cm (10 in × 8 in). Rococo ormolu plinth, 12¾ cm × 23 cm (5 in × 9 in). Round velvet covered, dark-plum-coloured base mat, 23 cm (9 in) in diameter.

EQUIPMENT
A round plastic bowl as a liner for the container, 15 cm × 9 cm (6 in × 3½ in). Block of well-soaked foam, fitting across the liner taped to it, standing 15 cm (6 in) above the rim of the container. Two pieces of tape securing the bowl to the container at the back.

FOLIAGE
Hosta fortunei 'Albopicta' (plantain lily).
Acer palmatum 'Atropurpureum'.
Pieris 'Forest Flame' *(P. forrestii)* (Andromeda).
Philadelphus coronarius 'Aurea' (mock orange).

FLOWERS
Aruncus dioicus (A. sylvester, A. vulgaris) (goat's beard).
Cornus kousa (Benthamidia japonica, Benthamia japonica) (dogwood).
Viburnum betulifolium (snowball).
Paeonia lactiflora 'Bowl of Cream' (double peony).
Carnations, lemon yellow.
Matthiola incana 'Excelsior' strain (column stock), cream and white.
Lilies 'Red Pirate' and 'Juliana'.
Roses, orange-red.

ARRANGER
Evelyn Mercer

THE RECEPTION

1 With the base, plinth and container in position, place the hosta leaves in a triangular form at the top and the sides of the block of foam, high on the right, lower on the left. Take a tall stem of aruncus and place this centrally, behind the topmost hosta. Add a flowing stem of cornus out to the left and viburnum to the right and in the front. With a third stem of viburnum take the design round towards the tapestry, placing this stem behind the cornus. Follow the established outlines with stems of acer.

2 Form a central band of rich colour with the pieris foliage and then add the cream peonies, starting above the top piece of pieris and curving their line slightly to the left, back to the centre and out again on the left. To the right-hand side add a stem of the bright yellow-leaved philadelphus.

3 Around the outside of the arrangement and to the right of the pieris, also between the two lowest peonies, add stems of aruncus. With the carnations include a little very pale yellow in the middle and to the right.

4 Take the stocks and add them at both sides, round towards the back of the design, high on the right and recessed a little on both sides of the pieris. On the right-hand side, place two stems of the orange-brown lilies. On the left, use three stems of the cream lilies, taking one round towards the back and the tapestry. Near the centre, just over the rim of the container, use two of the orange-red roses and another over to the right, below the lilies.

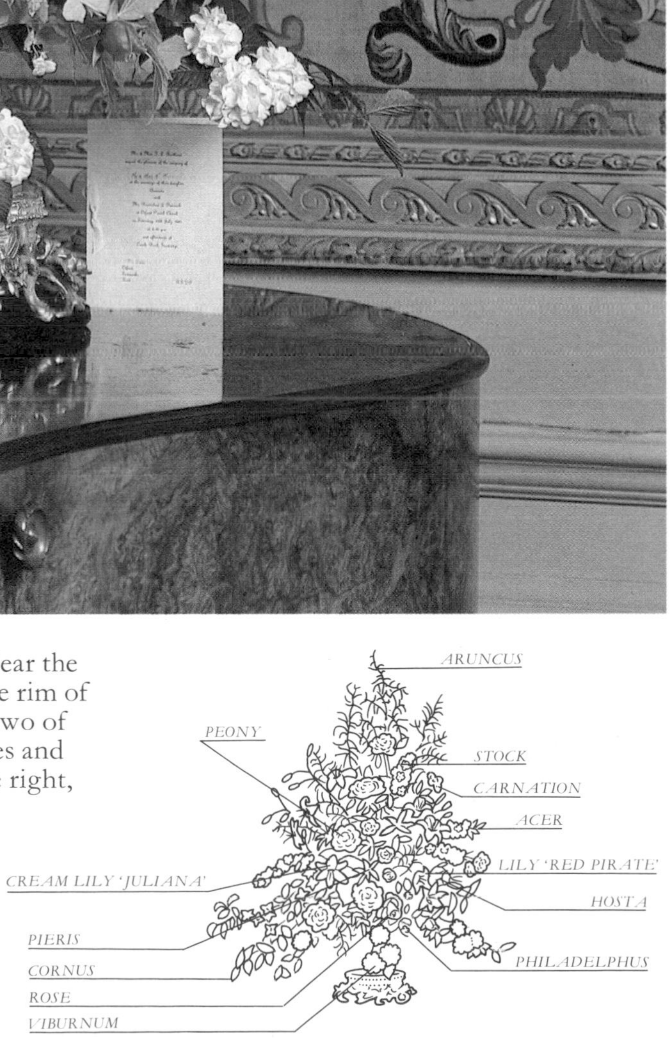

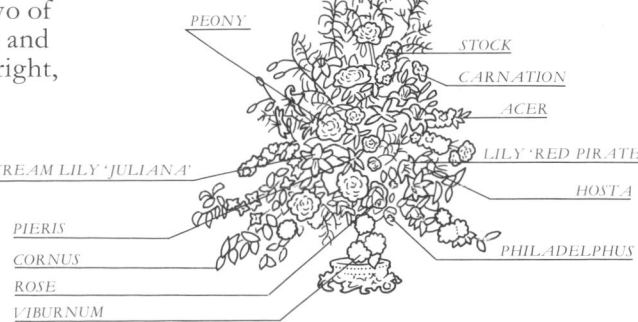

ARUNCUS
PEONY
STOCK
CARNATION
ACER
LILY 'RED PIRATE'
CREAM LILY 'JULIANA'
HOSTA
PIERIS
PHILADELPHUS
CORNUS
ROSE
VIBURNUM

THE TOAST

A LITTLE of the rich red in the room is repeated in this arrangement. It stands in front of doors open to the garden and the setting is ready for the speeches and the toast at this summer wedding reception.

SIZE
94 cm × 152 cm × 86 cm
(37 in × 60 in × 34 in).

CONTAINER
A matt gold-coloured bowl on a pedestal base, 28 cm × 18 cm (11 in × 7 in), standing on an oval base, covered in dull gold material, 30½ cm × 20 cm (12 in × 8 in).

EQUIPMENT
A block of soaked foam, cut to fit across the bowl and standing 5 cm above the rim (2 in), covered with 2½ cm (1 in) mesh wire netting.

FOLIAGE
Fagus sylvatica 'Riversii' (Rivers' Purple) (copper beech).
Euonymus japonicus 'Latifolius Albomarginatus' 'Latifolius Variegatus' ('Macrophyllus Albus') (Japanese spindle).
Stipa gigantea (feather or needle grass).
Hosta fortunei 'Albopicta'.
Primula japonica (Japanese primrose).

FLOWERS
Pyracantha coccinea (firethorn).
Iris spuria hybrid, 'Sierra Nevada'.
Alchemilla mollis (lady's mantle).
Hydrangea anomala petiolaris (climbing hydrangea).
Matthiola incana 'Excelsior' strain (column stock).
Alstroemeria 'Ligtu' hybrids (Peruvian lily).
Carnations.
Lilies 'Mont Blanc' and 'Red Pirate'.
Rose 'Circus'.

ARRANGER
Graeme Audrain

1 With long stems of copper beech, pyracantha and variegated euonymus, establish the lines of the arrangement along the table—beech forward to the left and back towards the right, pyracantha back on the left and euonymus forward on the right. Add four iris flowers in the middle, a tall stem surrounded by three shorter stems, not all exactly the same height. Around the iris add stems of the feathery grass.

2 Continue to work all round the arrangement (it will be seen from every angle). Place hosta leaves and primula leaves from the middle out over the rim of the bowl in groups of two or three at different levels and take a few hostas up into the centre to curve outwards a little. With sprays of alchemilla follow these curving leaves. Add some hydrangea heads in the heart of the arrangement and out over the rim of the container.

3 Add the cream stocks, two on the right quite high up and one low over the edge of the bowl. Add two more on the other side of the arrangement, low on the left. Tuck stems of the rich red alstroemeria in quite near the centre and then bring cream lilies across, from the left at the back to the centre, adding two red lilies a little lower down. Just to the right of

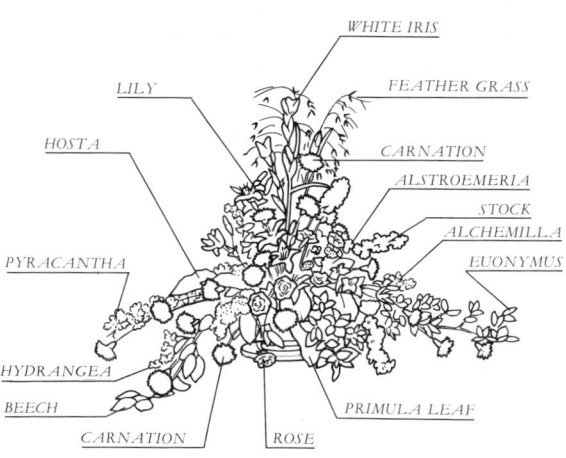

the centre, and repeated at the other side, place the very pale cream euonymus foliage.

4 Add both the crimson and the soft-orange carnations in flowing lines through the arrangement. Place a stem of the orange-red lily up to the left to balance the stocks on the right and finish the arrangement with the roses. Place these towards the centre and down over the rim of the container, making sure some are seen from whatever angle you view the arrangement.

WHITE IRIS

FEATHER GRASS

LILY

CARNATION

HOSTA

ALSTROEMERIA

STOCK

ALCHEMILLA

PYRACANTHA

EUONYMUS

HYDRANGEA

BEECH

PRIMULA LEAF

CARNATION

ROSE

FLOWERS AND leaves taken from a spring bride's bouquet have been carefully preserved, then re-assembled, mounted and framed.

SIZE
29 cm × 25½ cm (11½ in × 10 in), in a frame (not shown) 38 cm × 48 cm (15 in × 19 in).

BACKGROUND
Pale grey-green, matt finish material, pulled evenly over an oblong of hardboard and taped in place all round.

EQUIPMENT
Glue (latex type), tweezers and a magnifying glass. Ribbon.

FOLIAGE
Akebia quinata.
Ranunculus ficaria 'Flore Pleno' (double celandine).
Lonicera periclymenum 'Belgica' (early Dutch honeysuckle, woodbine).
Myosotis sylvatica (forget-me-not), preserved on the flower stems.
Violet leaf.

FLOWERS
Polygonum bistorta (knotweed, snakeweed), five.
Myosotis sylvatica (forget-me-not), ten.
Clematis montana rubens, five.
Primula auricula (auricula, dusty miller), one.
Primula veris (cowslip), two.
Ranunculus ficaria 'Flore Pleno' (double celandine), four.
Akebia quinata, two.
Bellis perennis (English daisy), two.
Viola odorata (sweet violet), one.
Rosa xanthina 'Canary Bird', buds, three.
Syringa microphylla (lilac), one spray.
Vinca major (greater periwinkle, blue-buttons), one.
Polyanthus *(Primula × polyantha, P. veris elatior, P. vulgaris elatior),* two.
Lonicera periclymenum 'Belgica' (early Dutch honeysuckle, woodbine), four.
Helleborus orientalis hybrid (Lenten rose), one complete flower and single petals.
Helleborus niger (Christmas rose), one.

All the plant material is preserved by the desiccant method.

ARRANGER
Dorothy Bye

MEMENTO

1 First arrange the plant material on a sheet of light-coloured paper, moving the pieces round until the design is satisfactory. Transfer it, bit by bit, to the background prepared earlier and glue each piece in position. It will be found easiest to keep the three-dimensional effect by working first with all the foliage which lies close to the background, then from the outside, finishing in the middle of the design. After lightly gluing the leaves in position add the polygonum, four at the top and one as the lowest piece of material on the right. Next use the forget-me-nots, eight stems round the outside and two clusters of flowers near the centre. Follow with clematis, from the top and round the design, continuing the triangular shape.

double celandines, again repeating the triangular lines. With two pieces of akebia add a little dark red on the left, then a daisy and a violet on the right, both curving down a little. Add more leaves in the middle of the design, remembering, as every piece of plant material is glued in position, to recess some and bring others forward just as in a fresh arrangement. Continue with the flowers, placing three yellow rosebuds, one by the daisy on the right, another looking down with its head over the curving line of the polygonum stem and a third to the left of this one. Add a second daisy on the left near the centre. A tiny spray of lilac added low on the left but above the celandine repeats the colour of the akebia.

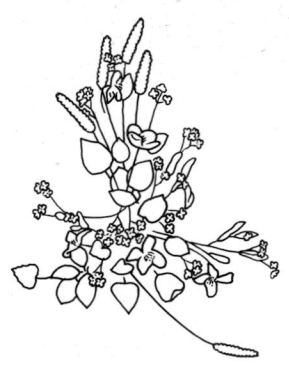

2 The auricula is the first of a number of yellow flowers which are added next. Place the auricula below the top clematis, the cowslips to right and left, and the

3 Work through the middle of the design with the larger flowers, starting with the periwinkle on the left just below the single cowslip. Add two yellow polyanthus flowers, one on the right opposite the periwinkle, the second by the spray of forget-me-nots on the left. Place a tight bud of honeysuckle above the lowest of the celandines on the right and another just below the polygonum on the left. Two sections of honeysuckle flower, used in front of the largest central leaf and halfway up the right-hand polygonum stem at the top, add interest without bulk.

4 Single petals of the purple-flowered hellebores can be curved round and glued into cup shapes. Prepare seven of these and use them behind the leaves on the right, tucked in above the lower rose, with the last two across the stem of the polygonum by the same rose. Finish the picture with two hellebore flowers and the ribbon. Place the darker hellebore a little higher and to the right of the periwinkle and the Christmas rose below it. Both flowers should look up towards the top right-hand corner rather than straight forward. Add the ribbon, never wider than $\frac{3}{5}$ cm ($\frac{1}{4}$ in), in curls and loops and short straight pieces to suggest the original bouquet.

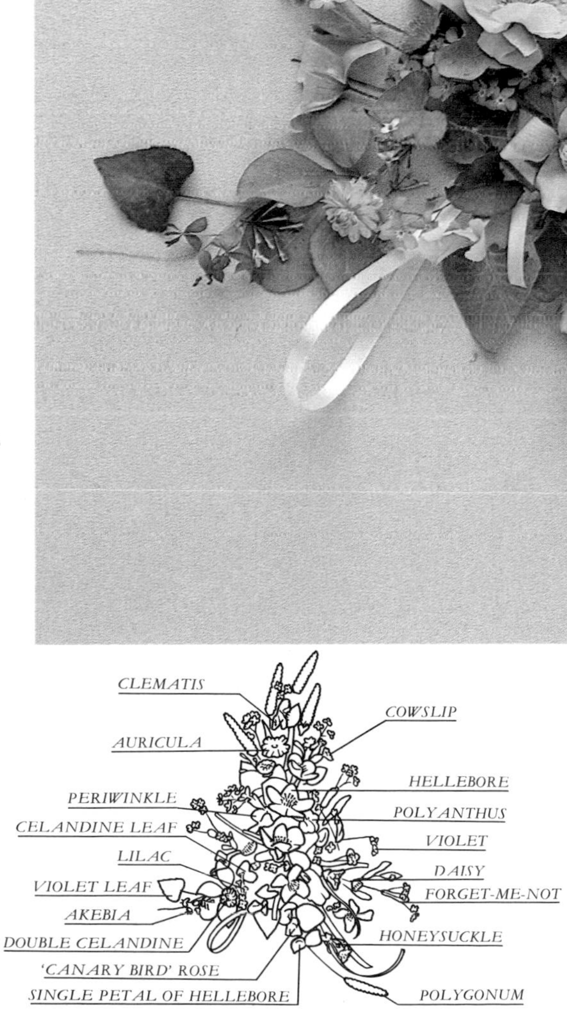

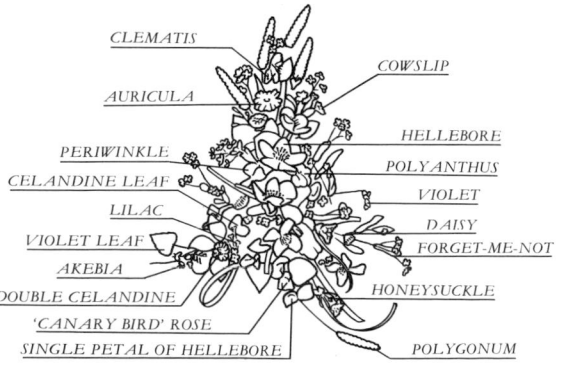

CLEMATIS
AURICULA
COWSLIP
HELLEBORE
PERIWINKLE
POLYANTHUS
CELANDINE LEAF
VIOLET
LILAC
DAISY
VIOLET LEAF
FORGET-ME-NOT
AKEBIA
DOUBLE CELANDINE
HONEYSUCKLE
'CANARY BIRD' ROSE
SINGLE PETAL OF HELLEBORE
POLYGONUM

Because this arrangement has been designed with flowers standing forward from the background it will need a deep, box-type frame. Make the picture air tight, covering it with glass and sealing it carefully. This will keep the flowers and leaves in good condition and help to preserve the colours.

103

FLOWERS IN A TEAPOY

STANDING IN front of an east-facing window, with the mill pool in view below, this Regency teapoy is filled with flowers from the garden, where the lawns go down to the river and banks of flowers rise behind the old mill.

The flowers are arranged in an apparently casual manner but it is no accident that the treasured teapoy is not overfilled and that the finished arrangement draws attention to the view.

SIZE
66 cm × 40½ cm (26 in × 16 in).

CONTAINER
The teapoy stands 96½ cm (38 in) high from the ground to the top of the open lid and is 40½ cm (16 in) wide.

EQUIPMENT
A soft green-coloured velvet base board 25 cm (10 in) in diameter. Round plastic dish, 15 cm (6 in) in diameter. Block of foam cut to fit and standing 7 cm (2¾ in) above the dish rim. Length of split cane.

FOLIAGE
Hosta undulata (plantain lily). Ribes sanguineum 'Brocklebankii' (golden-leaved flowering currant).

FLOWERS
Weigela 'Variegata' (Diervilla). Aquilegia × hybrida (columbine). Clematis montana. Tellima grandiflora (T. odorata) (fringecup). Syringa × josiflexa 'Bellicent' (lilac). Aquilegia vulgaris (columbine). Rosa 'Constance Spry' (early flowering modern shrub rose). Paeonia officinalis 'Rubra Plena' (peony). Alchemilla erythropoda (lady's mantle).

ACCESSORIES
Two small bronze dancers.

ARRANGER
Mary Watson

1 Remove the caddies and the mixing bowl from the teapoy and then place the green base to rest centrally on the back and front edges. Put the plastic dish in the middle and take the piece of cane, using it to prop the lid open at about a 45° angle (out of the foam and fitting under the lid edge). With the two stems of weigela suggest a diagonal line from the right down to the left. Add two more, one on the right to come over the front corner and one on the left, shorter than its neighbour and coming out over the front of the teapoy.

2 With two of the clearly marked and undulating hosta leaves, follow the first two placements of weigela. Take a third from the centre, out over the front of the teapoy and to the right, then place a little pink columbine flower at the top in the middle, just below the edge of the open lid. Below this, flowing right forward over the front, add a spray of *Clematis montana* and another out towards the window on the left. Add three of the delicate stems of tellima, one by the front hosta, one following the line of the hosta up on the right and the third by the second piece of clematis. Use stems of the golden-leaved currant in the centre of the arrangement where they will show up well against the dark wood and make a lively background for the larger flowers.

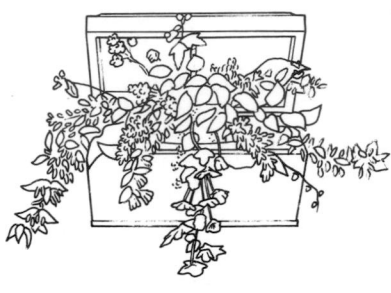

3 Add the lilac next, one spray behind the weigela on the left, one just to the left of the front spray of clematis, one by the tellima on the right and then one towards the back of the arrangement on either side. On the right-hand side, add pink columbines, higher at the back and tucked in near the lilac lower down. On the left, use a few blue ones where they will nod prettily in front of a pink rose; add another towards the front just below the lilac on the right. Put the roses in next. The one behind the blue columbines first and then the others down through the arrangement in an undulating line, the lowest one by the tellima and lilac on the right, five in all. Above the middle rose add one full blown peony. Here and there, with some short pieces of alchemilla, pick up the yellow of the currant leaves again.

Angle the teapoy slightly and put a little

figure on either side on the window-sill. This then is the view, coming into the room, of the flowers arranged in a favourite piece of furniture and with the willows and the mill pool beyond.

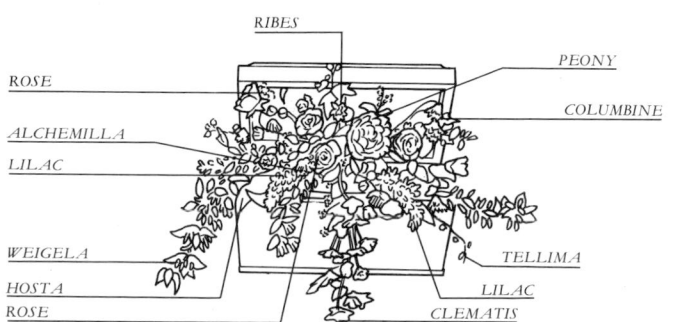

RIBES
ROSE
PEONY
ALCHEMILLA
COLUMBINE
LILAC
WEIGELA
TELLIMA
HOSTA
LILAC
ROSE
CLEMATIS

THE CHARM OF SMALL TREASURES

THE CHINA basket and the dainty plant material link together the intricate details of the decoration on the lamp base and cup and the more delicate painting on the tiny teapot. Scale plays its part, too, in this corner composition.

Pink and white flowers with yellow-green and brown-green leaves repeat the colours in the china and the marble of the table.

SIZE
30 cm × 15 cm (12 in × 6 in).

CONTAINER
White china basket with pale pink and green applied floral decoration, the handle set across from the right at the back to the left at the front. The feet repeat this curve. 15 cm × 12 cm (6 in × 5 in).

EQUIPMENT
An oblong of foam, two thirds filling the basket and coming a little higher than the rim.

FOLIAGE
Adiantum raddianum (delta maidenhair fern).
Tiarella cordifolia (foam flower).

FLOWERS
Pink spray carnations.
Cyclamen hederifolium (C. neapolitanum) (sowbread).
Cluster rose (Floribunda) 'Iceberg'.
Green and pink buds of antirrhinum (snapdragon).

ARRANGER
Felicity Bickley

1 Four graceful sprays of the fern are used, two out to the sides, one towards the right at the front and, a little higher but still lower than the handle of the basket, the fourth flowing out to the back at the left. These four sprays form the framework of the arrangement which is to be kept low but with depth from front to back so that it can be enjoyed from the front or when looking down into it.

2 The tiarella leaves are added in the middle and these, with the carnations, are placed diagonally across the design in the opposite direction to the handle.

3 The little cyclamen flowers are used to suggest the line of the handle and draw attention to the china flowers on the basket. 'Iceberg' roses are placed near the middle of the design and form a link with the white of the china. Antirrhinum buds are placed to follow the lines of the basket handle.

ANTIRRHINUM BUD

ROSE 'ICEBERG'

CARNATION

ADIANTUM

CYCLAMEN

TIARELLA LEAVES

HARMONY

THE BEAUTIFUL colours and the craftsmanship of the inlaid table, the dramatic vase and the repeating curves of the china dogs provide a setting for an arrangement, modest in size, almost triangular in shape and not, in any way, hiding the table or the treasures displayed on it. The colours in the china and the table are repeated in the cream, burnt-orange, soft green and red-brown of the flowers and leaves.

SIZE
38 cm × 15 cm (15 in × 6 in).

CONTAINER
Cut glass bowl, 11½ cm (4½ in) in diameter and 4 cm (1½ in) high.

EQUIPMENT
A square of well-soaked foam standing 4 cm (1½ in) above the rim.

FOLIAGE
Paeonia officinalis 'Rubra Plena' (cottage garden peony).

FLOWERS
Artemisia lactiflora (lad's love, southernwood).
Alstroemeria 'Ligtu Hybrids' (Peruvian lily).
Spray chrysanthemums 'Apricot Marvel'.

ARRANGER
Marjorie Watling

1 Form the outline with sprays of the cream-flowered artemisia. Place the tallest piece two thirds of the way back in the foam and the side pieces low down and coming slightly forward. Place short pieces over the rim of the bowl. The side pieces should be about a third longer than the tallest piece. Add single alstroemeria flowers.

2 Add a few pieces of the peony foliage to make a richly-coloured backing for the paler chrysanthemum flowers. Place these to repeat the lines of the artemisia, one flower at a time taken from the many-headed sprays.

3 Complete the design with a few more chrysanthemums and alstroemerias used at the front. Make the back and the sides of the arrangement attractive with more flowers and short sprays of artemisia but keep these low and tucked in so that they do not spoil the outline of the arrangement from the front.

CHRYSANTHEMUM
PEONY LEAF
ALSTROEMERIA
ARTEMISIA

BOOKS AND FLOWERS

AN ARRANGEMENT to complement the subtle tones of the leather and gold in the bindings of the books. The design is slender and asymmetrical and it stands on a circular table with a brass gallery.

Lime-green, grey-green, yellow, peach and a dull pink are the colours chosen to tone with the curtains and other furnishings in the room.

SIZE
76 cm × 43 cm (31 in × 17 in).

CONTAINER
A black marble plinth supports an urn. The plinth is decorated with a copper plaque depicting a goddess. The urn is 35 cm (14 in) high and 21 cm (8½ in) across the handles. A circular black wooden base from a Victorian glass dome is used under the container.

EQUIPMENT
A square piece of well-soaked foam and wire netting to cover.

FOLIAGE
Polygonatum × hybridum (P. multiflorum) (Solomon's seal).
Hydrangea macrophylla.

FLOWERS
Hydrangea macrophylla.
Peach coloured florists' gladioli.
Yellow dahlias.
Moluccella laevis (bells of Ireland).
Sedum telephium.

OTHER PLANT MATERIAL
Berries of *Sorbus hupehensis* 'Obtusa' (rowan, pink fruited) and of *Symphoricarpus* 'Constance Spry' (snowberry, pink tinted fruit). Seed-heads of *Curtonus paniculatus* (*Antholyza paniculata*) (Aunt Eliza, pleated leaves).

ARRANGER
Norah Phillippo

1 The foam is placed to come well above the rim of the container and is covered loosely with the wire netting which is attached carefully to the handles. Use three stems of Solomon's seal to establish the outline, together with three stems of bells of Ireland, the tallest of which is placed so that it forms a vertical line between the tallest, curving piece of Solomon's seal and the centre front of the plinth. Then add rosettes of hydrangea leaves to give weight in the centre and a small bunch of sorbus berries with a green hydrangea head to come over the edge of the urn at the front.

2 Next come three peach-coloured gladioli. One follows the established curve, another the vertical central line and the third, cut shorter, repeats the line on the left. Then tuck in slender branches of snowberries to soften the outline on the left. A pinkish-green hydrangea head can be positioned in the centre, and three yellow dahlias give stronger colour and shape where they restate the asymmetrical design.

3 Then add two more dahlias, one to emphasize the height and the other the depth on the right-hand side. Three sprays of curtonus seed-heads add interest and contrast. Place two more hydrangea heads near the centre and use the flowering sprays of the sedum, in the front on the right and towards the back on the left, to complete the arrangement.

CURTONUS SEED HEADS
GLADIOLUS
SNOWBERRY
MOLUCCELLA
DAHLIA
SORBUS
SOLOMON'S SEAL
SEDUM
HYDRANGEA LEAF
HYDRANGEA

DECORATIVE BOXES

GREEN AND gold autumn flowers and berries stand in a shaft of afternoon sunshine among a collection of interesting boxes.

The colours are complementary to the various woods used, the decorations of the boxes and the inlaid, low table on which they stand.

SIZE
22 cm × 11 cm (8½ in × 4½ in).

CONTAINER
Small round cut glass bowl with silver rim, 10 cm × 3½ cm (4 in × 1½ in).

EQUIPMENT
A square of well-soaked foam fitting the bowl firmly at the four points of contact and standing 2½ cm (1 in) above the rim.

FOLIAGE
Heuchera sanguinea (coral bells).

FLOWERS
Rosebuds from the cluster rose (Floribunda) 'Dainty Maid'.
Mignon dahlias.
Florists' apricot-coloured spray carnations.

OTHER PLANT MATERIAL
Berries of *Hypericum elatum* 'Elstead' (St. John's wort) and of *Pyracantha rogersiana* 'Flava' *(P. crenulata)* (firethorn).
Sprays of a tiny euphorbia (spurge).

ARRANGER
Felicity Bickley

1 Three heuchera leaves are placed in the foam, about 2 cm (1 in) from the edge and to come over the rim of the bowl. Place stems of pyracantha berries and sprays of euphorbia between the leaves.

2 Add single blooms from the sprays of carnations informally through the design. The rosebuds are added next to give a little height and a change of form above the rounded shapes of the other flowers, the berries and the leaves.

3 Tiny yellow mignon dahlias, hypericum berries and a few more of the pyracantha berries will complete the arrangement.

ROSEBUD CARNATION

EUPHORBIA

DAHLIA

PYRACANTHA

HYPERICUM HEUCHERA

THE WILD ONE

A MUCH-LOVED bronze, full of action, is complete and needs no embellishment, but the twists and curves of the branches seemed to share the dancing lines of the horse and a design evolved to suggest freedom and the joy of movement.

Set against the window, with the winter night outside, this became a study of darkness and light.

SIZE
81 cm × 71 cm (32 in × 28 in).

CONTAINER
A small, textured, modern pottery bowl 10 cm × 14 cm (4 in × 5½ in).

EQUIPMENT
Large pinholder.

FOLIAGE
Mahonia aquifolium (Oregon grape) and *Mahonia japonica,* both glycerined and then lightly sprayed with gold.

OTHER PLANT MATERIAL
A branch of *Lonicera periclymenum* (honeysuckle, woodbine) stripped of its bark, dried and lightly painted with brown and touched with white afterwards.
A branch of *Corylus avellana* 'Contorta' (corkscrew hazel) in its natural state.

ACCESSORY
The bronze horse.

ARRANGER
Mavis Brooker

1 Anchor the honeysuckle and hazel branches firmly on the pinholder before it is put in the container. Place the honeysuckle in an upright position and the hazel at an angle to the right but slightly forward.

2 Wire the *Mahonia aquifolium* leaves together and then attach them to come down in a curve on the right from the top of the honeysuckle. With the second spray of leaves, attached at a lower point, continue this curving line. On the left, arrange a balancing group of Mahonia leaves on the pinholder.

3 The setting complete, place the horse facing to the left, within, rather than out of, the circle suggested by the mahonia leaves on either side.

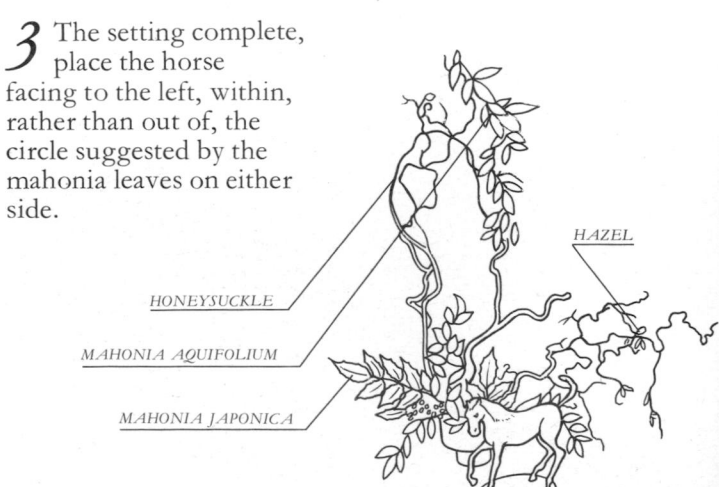

HAZEL

HONEYSUCKLE

MAHONIA AQUIFOLIUM

MAHONIA JAPONICA

LOOKING AFTER PLANT MATERIAL

When you bring cut stems of flowers, foliage and other plant material into your home they will be faced with a much drier atmosphere than they knew in the garden, the hot-house or the florist's shop and the following hints may help you to prolong the pleasure you have from your flower arrangements.

FROM THE GARDEN

It is wise to cut from the garden well before you intend to create your arrangements. The best times of the day for cutting, especially in hot weather, are first thing in the morning and in the evening as this is when transpiration is at its lowest. Ideally one should carry a bucket of water round the garden and put the stems in straight away, but this is not always convenient. However, it is essential to get the cut stems into water at the first possible moment.

Cutting the stems again under water does help to get rid of air-locks and opens up a fresh area which will absorb water much more readily than the already drying stem ends. Stems should be cut at a slight angle to give a larger drinking surface.

Many leaves and sprays of leaves can be completely submerged for a time and then stood upright in deep water until required. Grey foliage must never be submerged. The greyness is caused by the woolly surface of the leaves. When this becomes saturated and flattened, the greyness is lost and the by now felty, heavy leaves can siphon water out of a container with disastrous results for both the arrangement and the furniture.

Having cut the stems and placed them in deep, cold water, find a cool spot for the buckets. In very hot weather a stone or cement floor can be a great help and if it is possible to throw water over the floor this, as it evaporates, creates a certain amount of moisture around the petals and the leaves. In the case of very cold weather a frost-free place must be found.

Leave the stems in water for several hours, overnight is ideal. It will mean that the plant material has time to become fully charged with water and will be more likely to last well when it is used in a warm, dry room.

Preparing the mechanics for your arrangements is covered on page 122 but it is worth mentioning here the need to have your container ready before taking your plant material out of the buckets. It should not be away from a water supply any longer than is essential.

FROM THE FLORIST

The same treatment is appropriate for flowers and foliage purchased from a florist but a few additional facts should be remembered.

During winter, flower markets can be very cold and the cut blooms, leaves and pot plants may have come from warmer climates or from conditions of high humidity needed to encourage quick growth. After leaving the grower they endure transport by air, sea, road or rail before reaching a possibly draughty market. Then another journey follows to the selling point from where you, the final owner, will take them on yet another journey.

Most florists keep their stock in satisfactory and cool conditions and, where appropriate, will give the bunches a good long drink before they are sold. They will, however, still need care when you get them home. The ends should be re-cut before putting the stems in water for a few hours. This will give them time to recover before being put into relatively shallow water and a warm room. Try to keep all plant material away from direct heat or any draughts.

CASES FOR SPECIAL TREATMENT

Cold conditions can retard the opening of some flowers and the most satisfactory way to encourage buds to open is to use tepid water in the bucket and to place this in a warm but not hot atmosphere.

Stems cut from garden shrubs, for instance forsythia or *Prunus triloba* (double cherry), can be hurried into premature flowering by being given the same gentle warmth. Research has shown that forsythia does need a prolonged period of cold weather before it will respond in this way and warm winter weather could be the reason for occasional failure.

Some flowering trees and shrubs have leaves which absorb all the water when they are picked, leaving the flowers in a wilted state very soon after gathering. Examples of these are syringa (lilac) and philadelphus (mock orange). Remove the leaves at once; perhaps a few small leaves can be left here and there, but if more than a very few remain the flowers will wilt quickly.

Plants with a milky sap, for instance poppies and euphorbias (spurge), will not last unless the stems are sealed as soon as they are cut. This is done by singeing which only takes a second or two, and then the stems must go into deep water for a while. Beware of some of these milky saps, they can cause severe irritation to the skin.

Some flowers cut from bulbs do not like deep water, the narcissus family in particular. Give them a drink in about two inches of water and then arrange them in shallow water on pin-holders. Tulips do benefit from being wrapped fairly tightly in paper, up to their necks, and stood in deep water for a long drink. This encourages them to hold themselves erect and not wander into interesting curves just as soon as they are arranged. However, their wilfulness has its own charms and adds a naturalness to arrangements in our own homes.

Anemones, especially the florists' varieties, De Caen and St. Brigid, and forced roses have a habit of drooping badly. Revive them by putting them into a narrow container, again up to their necks, in very hot water. The petals must be protected from the steam. An improvement should be noticed quite quickly but leave them in this water until it is cold, by which time they should be fully recovered. They prefer being arranged on pin-holders and in wire netting rather than foam which tends to clog the stems.

New spring foliage is particularly difficult to condition and quite different from the mature leaves you will pick later in the season. Handle it very carefully and give it as long as possible in deep water, but it is unwise to try to use very fragile new leaves.

It is worth remembering that any plant which flowers or produces new leaves in the cold months of the year must enjoy cool conditions and it will find a hot, dry, indoor atmosphere very much more difficult to cope with than flowers which have their season in the warm weather or mature leaves which have developed a more leathery quality.

ADDITIONAL METHODS OF CONDITIONING

One way to make sure that the plant material which is most difficult to condition will last is to use the boiling water method. Put about 5 cm (2 in) of water in a small pan and bring it to a rolling boil. Hold the tips of the stems in the boiling water for a few seconds, the time depending upon the toughness or otherwise of the stem. For instance, a very soft stem will only need the time it takes you to count to five, a slightly tougher stem till ten and a tough one till twenty. Experience will teach you how fast you should count. While doing this, protect the petals and the leaves from the steam and, as soon as the stems have been treated, plunge them into deep

cold water for a further drink. Only treat a few stems at a time or you will find you over-cook some and miss others.

Removing the surplus thorns from the lower part of rose stems and other thorny subjects will allow them to drink more easily and, especially with purchased hot-house roses, remove some of the leaves or they will drink more than their share of the water. It helps to split the stems of roses carefully and also of other subjects with tough or woody stems but smashing is not a good idea, it just makes the water foul and the stems difficult to arrange. Any leaves which will be below the surface of the water, or where they will make it difficult to get the stems into the foam, pin-holder or wire-netting, should be removed.

Cleaning the surface of smooth, shiny leaves is worth doing as it removes unsightly and clogging dirt and dust. This can be done with damp cotton wool or a tissue but care must be taken not to damage the surface. There are proprietary products on the market for adding a sheen to leaves and it is possible to use oil or milk, but whatever is used it should be with restraint. A leaf which looks oily is neither attractive nor able to breathe and more dust will settle on the oil.

Berries and seed-heads are interesting additions to many arrangements and, generally, they are trouble-free. Sometimes seed will drop out of pods sooner than is wished. *Iris foetidissima* (Gladwin iris) is an example with its brilliant orange-red berries which do tend to drop in a warm room. A spray-over with a firm-hold hair lacquer may stop this.

Many plants with wind carried seeds, the clematis family for one, have interesting seed-head formations which may be held with hair lacquer. A much more satisfactory method for clematis seed-heads is to preserve them with a glycerine mixture (see page 119) this will change the leaves to a rich brown and the seed-heads to a silky greyish brown.

A few hollow-stemmed flowers, like delphiniums, will repay having their stems filled with water and then plugged with cotton wool or a piece of foam.

AFTER-CARE

Spraying finished arrangements with water, creating moisture in the atmosphere around the arrangement, is a great help but it is not really practical where there is polished furniture or soft furnishings.

An arrangement should be checked at least once a day to see if it has sufficient water. It is surprising how often it will need topping-up, especially when a shallow container has been used. The first day, when the plant material is fully charged with water from the earlier careful conditioning, there may not be much lowering of the water level but after that, winter or summer, it will need frequent attention. Foam, once it is dry, is very difficult to re-wet and so it is necessary to leave adequate and easily found spaces between the foam and the container for this re-filling. The tip of a finger held just below the rim will be the best guide, telling you exactly when to stop pouring, but you must let the foam soak up as much water as it will, little by little, before you stop this re-filling process.

Wherever there is air conditioning, the life of flower arrangements can be drastically reduced and repeated checking is needed, with generous spraying and deep containers being the greatest help.

Although it may be time-consuming, the care taken in the preparation of all the plant material you use will mean that the arrangements stay fresh and give pleasure for much longer.

PRESERVING PLANT MATERIAL

It is useful to have a stock of preserved flowers, leaves and seed-heads for use when fresh plant material is scarce or for where central heating or air conditioning dries out the atmosphere—and also fresh petals and leaves—very quickly.

There is no need for dried arrangements to be dull for there are many contrasting shapes, textures and colours which can be used. It is, however, only too easy to collect a mass of preserved material and then use it indiscriminately just because it is there, ending up with a mixture which is far from satisfying, either because the colouring is monotonous or because the various shapes do not stand out clearly against one another or against the chosen background.

The colour range of preserved flowers is full of interest and possibilities. When flowers are dried carefully they have muted but pleasing colours and leaves and seed-heads can be preserved to provide all the tints, tones and shades of brown, from palest cream to a dark peat-brown. *Moluccella laevis* (bells of Ireland), green when fresh, will glycerine well and if bleached by sunlight afterwards will become a pale cream. *Aucuba japonica* (spotted laurel) glycerines to a very dark brown and *Fagus sylvatica* (green beech) can be picked two or three times during the mid-to-late summer and each batch will glycerine to a different shade. *Briza maxima* (quaking grass) air-dries to a pale parchment colour, seed-heads of the crocosmias (montbretias) keep some of their orange colour and iris seed pods dry to a medium brown but, if they are treated with glycerine, become much darker.

Many grey seed-heads and some grey flowers, or bracts, dry well. *Stachys lanata* (lamb's ears or woolly betony) and the artemisias (wormwood or mugwort) are examples and *Eucalyptus gunnii* (gum tree) leaves become an attractive purple-grey when treated with glycerine. By contrast, *Sorbus aria* (whitebeam) leaves turn brown on top but remain grey beneath. Rose foliage can be preserved by the glycerine method but it must be cut with some mature stems; it will be a very dark green when it has absorbed the glycerine mixture. A lighter green can be achieved with ferns which can be pressed. Bracken, picked before it curls but when it has its autumn colour, will be golden when it has been pressed.

Achillea filipendulina (yarrow) and many other yellow-flowered members of this family, keep their colour well when air dried and *Delphinium ajacis* (larkspur) is an example of a flower which will dry to a muted version of its fresh colour.

These are a very few examples of the many flowers and leaves which can be preserved, by one method or another, to show the range of colour and of form which the flower arranger can collect and use in arrangements for the home.

METHODS
There are several ways to preserve plant material. Air drying, using a glycerine mixture, pressing and using desiccants will be explained here. Freeze drying is becoming more common and is used commercially. A few plants dry best if they are arranged in shallow water and left in a dry but not too warm place. Hydrangea heads are an example and these should be picked when they start to feel crisp to the touch. When they are completely dry they will be quite papery but they will have kept their lovely colours.

AIR DRYING
Material for drying by this method should be just

coming to maturity, not too young, when the stems will tend to be rather limp, or too old, when the tendency may be for the flowers to fall apart. All plant material should be picked during a dry spell of weather. Air drying can be used for some leaves but most shrivel and become unattractive. Heavy textured leaves, such as those of aspidistra, strelitzia and hosta, take on interesting curves as they dry but leaving them in shallow water, as for the hydrangea heads, is likely to be more satisfactory, especially for the hosta leaves.

1. Deal with plant material as soon as it has been picked.
2. Strip surplus leaves off stems before bunching and tying together.
3. Bunch in fairly small quantities to avoid damaging the flowers.
4. Stems shrink as they dry so tie them up fairly tightly and check the bunches after a few days.
5. Hang the bunches up, heads downwards, in an airy, dry and, if possible, dark place. This ensures speedy drying and keeping a good colour.

GLYCERINE METHOD

Again the plant material should be picked when it is coming to maturity, and during a dry spell of weather. Old or wet plant material will take up the solution more slowly and there will be a tendency for mildew to form. Cut ends dry out quickly so pick and then deal with a few stems at a time. Leaves which have taken on their autumn colours cannot be preserved by this method. Glycerined material is much more supple to use than air dried stems.

1. Make up a glycerine mixture using one third of glycerine to two thirds of boiling water.
2. Stir thoroughly and use at once.
3. Fill fairly narrow jars to a depth of about 8 cm (3 in).
4. Place the newly cut stems, a few to a jar. This way they should drink the solution quickly. Too many stems in one jar may mean there is not enough solution and the plant material shrivels before this is noticed. Too many stems can also result in crushed and unattractive results.
5. Stems will take up the solution if it is cold when they are put in, but the process will be slower.
6. Stand the jars in a dry, airy place, out of strong light.
7. The length of time taken by various kinds of plant material varies, but it is ready when it has taken on an interesting colour and is very slightly oily to the touch. A few days will be long enough for some

material, two to three weeks for beech leaves, and much longer for heavy textured leaves such as those of aspidistra. Wipe over heavy leaves with the mixture as soon as they are picked to prevent them from drying out before they have taken up the solution. Some small, leathery leaves can be submerged until they are preserved.

8. Any solution which is left can be re-used.
9. Bleached effects can be achieved by standing the newly preserved material in a sunny window for a few days.
10. Dry storage is essential. This material can be packed in boxes ready for use.
11. Dusty and tired arrangements give no pleasure, but glycerined material can be refreshed by being wiped over with a soapy cloth and then dried carefully. Steaming for a few seconds will allow a little re-shaping but, again, it must be dried well before being used or stored.
12. When preserved material is used with fresh, the ends of the preserved stems should be dipped into something which will waterproof them, such as varnish.

DESICCANTS

Several types of desiccants can be used for preserving flowers, and leaves can also be treated in this way. Their purpose is to absorb moisture as quickly as possible and to leave a completely dry but brightly coloured flower which will hold its petals exactly as it did when it was picked.

Some desiccants are of a coarser grain than others. Sand is the heaviest and this must be washed and dried several times before it is used to remove impurities. Silica gel is less coarse and alum is finer. Borax is very fine and light; it does tend to clog on the petals but a mixture of sand and borax can be useful. The size and texture of the flower will suggest which will be the most suitable. The more delicate the flower the lighter the desiccant needed. After use, the desiccant must be thoroughly dried before it can be used again.

For this method airtight containers are necessary, their size and depth depending on the plant material to be dried in this way.

1. Put a layer of desiccant in the container to a depth of about 3 cm (1 in).
2. Place the bloom on top (no stem left on) and cover very carefully with desiccant, teasing it into every space between the petals so that each one is fully supported.
3. Add more desiccant to a depth of a further 2 cm ($\frac{3}{4}$ in).
4. Close and seal the container and leave it for a few days before examining. The flower should be dry and papery, if not it must go back in the desiccant for a little longer. If left too long it will become very fragile.

5 Dry and careful storage is essential.

Flowers preserved in this way have a charm which is particularly useful when making pictures and plaques. There are examples on pages 68 and 102.

PRESSED PLANT MATERIAL

A specially made flower press is helpful but not essential equipment for preserving plant material in this way. Heavy books can be used successfully if sheets of blotting paper are placed on either side of the flowers and leaves. Use markers to show what is being pressed and exactly where it is and then it will not be necessary to disturb the rest of the contents.

The most successful material for pressing is thin in texture and, of course, it should be dry when it is picked.

1 Remove stems and, if required, press them separately.
2 Press single petals rather than whole flowers if they are bulky.
3 Include leaves of many shapes and sizes, tendrils and grasses.

4 Use sufficient weight to force the moisture out into the blotting paper quickly.
5 Large flat leaves, such as ferns, can be pressed with a cool iron, placing them between sheets of blotting paper first. This starts the drying process quickly. They should be put under heavy weights afterwards.

Some flowers and leaves dry out quickly but their colours will hold better if they are left in a book or press for a long period; six months is not too long. When they are to be assembled into tiny arrangements or pictures, a pair of tweezers will be helpful for the smallest pieces and if glue is needed, a latex type is recommended.

Arrangements of preserved material are best assembled using pinholders, with or without wire netting, or one of the specially made dry foam blocks. These do not absorb moisture from the atmosphere but they are very light and so need to be securely anchored to containers.

Examples of preserved plant material used in arrangements can be seen in *Oak Parlour* (page 58), *The Whatnot* (page 12) and *The Wild One* (page 114).

CONTAINERS, BASES AND ACCESSORIES

When we arrange flowers for our own homes we turn to our favourite containers, knowing they will look well in certain places and that the finished arrangements will be complementary to their surroundings. Occasionally it is stimulating to try something different.

Many different materials are used to make attractive, interesting or curious containers and the choice can be confusing, but assembling a personal collection is fascinating. Some will add a great deal to a finished design and others will be merely practical ways of providing the plant material with a water supply, not seen at all.

CHOOSING A CONTAINER

Flower arrangements should add to but never overwhelm their settings. Size, style, colour and texture all play an important part in the finished picture, and so deciding which container to use is an early and interesting step in planning a design. For example, rough textures and strong shapes, perhaps of modern pottery, will be used in very different settings from a delicate porcelain vase

made in the 18th century. Carved wood may be successful with an arrangement of dried flowers and heavy seed-pots but where it is to stand will be equally important.

Alabaster vases are favourites with flower arrangers but water will damage them very quickly and properly fitted liners must be used. Silver scratches easily but, like so many metals, it is lovely with flowers and its gleaming surface is quite different from the bright shine of brass, the warmth suggested by copper, the rich tone of bronze or the softer finish of pewter. All have a place in the flower arranger's cupboard.

Glass has a special sparkle; cut or plain, coloured or clear, traditional or modern, the choice is enormous. In complete contrast there are baskets, usually simple in shape, varying in colour and texture but lending themselves well to flowers arranged with a matching simplicity.

SHALLOW CONTAINERS

Many arrangements are designed so that the container does not show and for these a variety of dishes, bowls or tins, many found in the kitchen cupboards, may be used, or there are specially made plastic dishes designed to hold water-retaining foam. Oblongs, rounds or ovals are all useful shapes but none should be very deep or they will be difficult to hide satisfactorily. Careful testing before they are used is a wise precaution as some of the more mundane items may leak, tins especially, and some pottery which has not been fired at a high temperature will remain porous.

Shiny tins can be made less obvious if they are given a coat of dark, matt-finish paint and garish decorations on cheap pottery can be dealt with in the same way.

When plant material is used to hide these shallow containers it may be responsible for siphoning water out of the arrangement on to the furniture. Grey, hairy-surfaced leaves are very likely to do this but almost any plant material will siphon if it lies across the rim of the container. Placing the stems at a slightly greater angle away from the rim and leaving these stems long enough to come forward and down without touching it, in an easy curve, is the solution to this problem, also it will give a much more natural flow to the leaves while still hiding the container from view.

LININGS FOR CONTAINERS

Valuable containers must be cared for, and using suitable linings will help. These need not be very grand and, once more, a look through the kitchen cupboards should solve most problems. Kitchen foil may be helpful but not if wire netting is to be used. Sometimes linings have a tendency to move around while the arrangement is being assembled or, disconcertingly, to swing over, face downwards, after it is finished. This can be caused by the flower stems becoming heavier when they are fully charged with water. It certainly means that the liner is not securely anchored and the arrangement is less than perfectly balanced.

Shallow bowls and dishes can be used as liners inside baskets and one should be chosen which is not too large. One no more than half the length of the basket will be adequate. In the same way, a flat-based dish can be raised up inside a trough, perhaps on a brick, and this makes it much easier to arrange the flowers and foliage in a natural and flowing way. If the whole trough or basket is filled from end to end with plant material the result will be a large and ungainly arrangement, smothering the container.

STEMMED CONTAINERS

Large flower stands, or pedestals, are very popular and useful. Some are attractive but others, in particular those made from very light-weight metal, can look unbalanced if they are used for large arrangements; however, they are pleasantly light for carrying around.

Most specially made pedestals have fixed containers on top, designed to take a good supply of foam or large, heavy pinholders and wire netting. They should be large enough to hold plenty of water as well as the chosen 'mechanics' because they are intended for arrangements of considerable size with a wealth of plant material. If, however, the top is flat, as it will be with many of the attractive wooden stands which can be found, then a suitable dish must be attached firmly and with care. Wood, marble, wrought iron, brass and even stone are all used for flower stands.

Figurines holding flowers aloft, candlesticks with flowers instead of candles (often both) and many other items, either designed for the purpose or adapted, can be used to raise flowers up and away from the furniture. Sometimes, as for buffet tables, this is for practical as well as for visual reasons but often the arranger will feel a more airy and delicate design can be created which will suit the setting and the flowers.

There is a halfway stage between this type of arrangement and flowers placed at table level in a low container and many of the containers used for this are based on the classical shapes of urns, vases and tazzas. Good examples will be very elegant and the arranger should not allow the flowers to detract from the good proportions or cover the interesting features which first made this chosen container seem right for its setting. Why use a beautiful container if it is not to be seen and enjoyed?

BASES

Putting a base under a container is a practical idea as it should protect the furniture but, if it is well chosen, it can add to the visual balance of the design. This does not mean that every flower arrangement should be provided with a base, far from it. It is just another feature that can be used where it is suitable.

Many bases are simple shapes covered with material. Plain rather than patterned fabrics are most likely to be successful. Hessian or a slightly stretchy nylon velvet are two examples of fabrics which give different finishes and are not too difficult to handle. Colours, light or dark, muted or bright and shapes and thicknesses are a matter of choice. The style of the container, the colours of the flowers and the size of the finished arrangement are all factors to be considered when deciding if a base should be used. Decide also whether it is to be used for extra impact or just as a quiet, toning addition.

Making fabric-covered bases is quite simple and round or oval shapes are most frequently used. Cake boards make good bases and come in various sizes and thicknesses, the thinnest being satisfactory for small arrangements which would be 'over-based' with a thicker one. Ovals can be cut from various compressed boards, a depth of about 1½ cm (½ in) being about right for most arrangements. A large arrangement may look best with more than one base of this kind rather than a very thick one.

These shapes are covered by carefully stretching and then gluing the material in place, making the underside tidy and smooth with more of the material or a firm paper. A lumpy finish on either side of the base will add nothing to the appearance of the arrangement or its balance.

Another way to make covers for these bases is to thread thin elastic cord through a narrow hem of material cut to the shape of the base. This should be about 8 cm (3 in) larger than the base itself. The finished 'mob-cap' can be slipped over and smoothed in place. This method means that the same board can be used with a number of covers but it does not work well with bulky material.

Other, more ingenious, shapes can be made to go with special containers and an example can be seen on page 80 (*Twenty-fifth Anniversary*). Patience is needed to cut out and cover such a shape satisfactorily.

Wooden bases may be slices of wood straight from the saw-mill, smoothed but left in their natural state or they can be stained and polished. A stock of many different grains and colours can be collected.

Small carved or lacquered stands are treasures worth looking for. Wooden trays are useful and some, with level tops, can be reversed and will give a pleasant block-type base. Indeed, trays of many kinds can be used, their different styles and materials suiting different settings.

Both marble and slate make interesting bases, but there is the problem of weight and protecting the surfaces upon which they are to stand (felt glued on is one solution). Mats of rush, grass or wicker are also worth considering.

TREASURES

Although accessories are most often thought of in competitive flower classes it is pleasant to incorporate special treasures with flowers at home, either as accessories or as the sole reason for placing an arrangement in a certain spot.

A favourite ornament or a collection of treasures can suggest a certain style or colour for an arrangement which will stand nearby, and it is for the flower arranger to find pleasure in linking the two, creating a complete and satisfying picture. Examples showing different approaches are found on pages 104–114. In *The Wild One*, the bronze was the whole reason for the design. In *Books and Flowers*, the beautiful mellow bindings of the books in the corner of the library suggested the colours and the design of that arrangement.

EQUIPMENT

Over the centuries flowers have been brought indoors and arranged for the joy of their colour, form and perfume and many are the ways in which they have been held in place.

Vases for single blooms, the more complicated bough or tulip pots, the wonderful selection of elegant narrow-necked vases, the *epergnes* and March stands, have all been designed to solve the problem of displaying flowers to the best possible advantage.

Sand and stones, twigs and bunches of greenery, moss, glass 'roses', marbles, metal grids and twisted strips of lead have all had their fashions and their followers. Floating flower heads in shallow dishes of water solved the problem for the hostess of the 1920s and 1930s but, more recently, wire netting (chicken wire), pin-holders and special water-retaining foams

have been used successfully and these 'mechanics' are described here. Although methods may vary, the purpose does not; it is to provide a secure and, if possible, invisible method of placing and holding stems exactly where the arranger has decided they should be.

FOAM

Throughout this book the most frequently used aid is foam, by itself or in conjunction with other equipment. It is made of highly absorbent material which is soft and somewhat crumbly, dull green in colour when dry and becoming darker and brighter when wet. It is widely available in brick-shaped blocks and in smaller rounds and squares. These smaller pieces are designed for plastic dishes with deeper central wells into which they fit. Special plastic containers can be found which are able to take larger blocks also.

It is important to make sure the foam is fully charged with water before it is used but it is not wise to leave it soaking for a long period before it is needed as this makes it more likely to disintegrate. A good guide is to soak it somewhere large enough for it to sink when it is full of water, then to take it out and to use it straight away. By the time the arrangement is complete the flowers will be drinking from it and the drying out will have started so it is essential to make sure the container is topped up and that the foam has stopped drinking again. If the foam does dry out once it has been soaked it is very difficult to get it to re-absorb water. It needs handling with some care as rough treatment, especially when it is wet, will break it up. Foam placed horizontally will drink water much more satisfactorily than if it is used in an upright position.

A strong piece of wire or a knife will cut through it easily, wet or dry, and assessing how much is needed for an arrangement is not difficult.

Although the foam needs to be anchored firmly, a container should not be filled entirely as there must be an easily found space for adding more water.

If a square or oblong of foam is placed on top of the container and pressed down lightly it will leave a mark which can be cut round, or the block can be pressed firmly into place with the surplus falling away. Some depth of the block should be left standing above the rim so that stems can be placed in it at an angle, to flow down over the edge where needed. The amount left standing proud will depend on the size of the arrangement and the quantity of plant material to be used.

Small arrangements may not need any further securing but for larger arrangements, or for where the foam cannot be wedged securely, additional 'mechanics' are needed.

Special tape can be bought which sticks to dry surfaces or to itself and is used as tape would be on a parcel.

Wire netting can be fitted over the top of the foam for added security but it must be fixed well, either to part of the container or with thin wire, tape, string or elastic bands, again like a parcel. The wire netting will damage the foam if it is not used carefully. The size of mesh is a matter of choice: $2\frac{1}{2}$ cm (1 in) 5 cm (2 in). The smaller gauge is stronger and is better for large arrangements where heavy stems are to be used. The two-inch mesh is easier to handle but it will dig into the foam more readily. It is also important to make sure the wire does not damage the container and it should not be used with any delicate surfaces.

Foam can be used with specially made holders. These are plastic and have prongs on which the foam is impaled. Fixing these to the container is done with a special putty-like substance but hands and container must be absolutely dry for success. A pinholder can be used in the same way but cleaning it afterwards is tedious.

Repeatedly taking stems in and out of the foam will mean that its life is shortened. If a heavy stem is too long and needs shortening it is better to cut it off at foam level and then place it again rather than to pull it out leaving a large hole. Pushing stems right through the foam defeats the object by weakening the block and the only occasion for doing this might be when, in a mixed arrangement, a few flowers are to be included which do not last well in foam. Carefully placing them so that they are taking up water from below is possible, but another method is to form a small 'well' for the stem using a slightly larger stalk and making sure this hole has filled with water.

Dry foam is similar in appearance but, as the name suggests, it does not absorb water. It is designed for arrangements of dried plant material, Christmas designs and others when water is not necessary. Usually it is green but some is produced in a dull grey-brown which is particularly useful for preserved plant material. Dry foam comes in various styles and sizes, brick-shapes, rounds, spheres and cones being the most usual. Particular attention must be paid to fixing this dry foam because it is very light. The same methods apply as above.

When using foam of any kind it is well to remember that too much will be difficult to hide and too little will make creating a graceful arrangement very difficult—stems will be overcrowded and the foam will fall apart. For designs which rely on very little but heavy or bold plant material for their success, foam is rarely satisfactory. A heavy pinholder is more likely to work well.

WIRE NETTING

Wire netting has been mentioned earlier. It can be used on its own but it must be fixed very firmly to the container or it will slide around maddeningly as each stem is added. The two-inch mesh is best in this case. If you fold it in three layers and then press it into approximately the shape of the inside of the container, a crumpled mass is provided into which the stems can be placed. The results are likely to be more casual than when using other methods but this suits many flowers and settings very well. Deep containers can be half-filled with sand or pebbles before fixing the wire or foam and this is a way of solving the problem of angling stems and of balance when heavy stems are used in tall narrow pots. A pinholder can be added underneath the wire and then some of the stems can be placed more firmly, and certainly more quickly.

PINHOLDERS

Pinholders come in rounds and oblongs and in many sizes. They are made of heavy metal bases with sets of sharp, upward-pointing pins. The width between the pins and the gauge of metal used for them varies and suitable pinholders can be found for plant material from the very delicate to the heavy. Used carefully they will last for years. Well-type pinholders hold a small supply of water round their pins.

When fixing a heavy branch onto a pinholder it is helpful to attach it lightly and then bang the pinholder on the floor so that the pins go up into the branch; in this way less damage is done to the pins. Taking the branch off again should be done with care for the same reason.

Stems can be set on the pins at any angle just so long as the drinking tip is below the water level.

Sometimes it is necessary to add a balancing weight at the back of a large arrangement and this can be done with an upturned pinholder fixed into the back pins of the one used for the arrangement.

OTHER EQUIPMENT

Other accessories, such as heavy bases with screw fittings to hold heavy branches, are available. Using one of these does save wear and tear on pinholders but they need a flat surface and they take up space within the arrangement so they are not always easy to incorporate.

Cones are useful additions to the flower arranger's box of equipment. They are made of metal or plastic, are usually green and can be used by pressing the pointed end into foam, wire or on pinholders. Alternatively, they can be taped securely to canes which are then used as upright stems in the arrangement. A small piece of crumpled wire or well-soaked foam is used inside the cones and one or two stems can be placed high up in the design. Topping up must not be forgotten as they will dry out fairly quickly.

Large scale 'mechanics' are a separate subject and outside the scope of this book. They are found most often in exhibitions and festivals. However, they are constructed of similar materials, mostly wire and foam, and arrangers enjoy designing and constructing their own 'mechanics' for every new and challenging exhibit.

Time spent in the preparation is not wasted. It is disheartening to see an arrangement fall apart as soon as it is finished and always a pleasure to arrange flowers knowing that the 'mechanics' are secure and well balanced.

INDEX